knitting
wizardry

27
Spellbinding Projects

Amy Clarke Moore

INTERWEAVE
interweave.com

EDITOR
Erica Smith

TECHNICAL EDITORS
Tracey Davidson, Karen Frisa, Amanda Kirk,
Alexandra Virgiel

PHOTOGRAPHER
Nathan Rega of Harper Point

PHOTO STYLING
Allie Liebgott, Ann Sabin Swanson

HAIR + MAKEUP
Kathryn MacKay

ASSOCIATE ART DIRECTOR
Charlene Tiedemann

COVER DESIGN
Jason Reid

INTERIOR DESIGN
Adrian Newman

PRODUCTION
Kerry Jackson

Interweave
A division of F+W Media, Inc.
4868 Innovation Drive
Fort Collins, CO 80525
interweave.com

Manufactured in the United States by Roanoke

Library of Congress Cataloging-in-Publication Data

Knitting wizardry : 27 spellbinding projects /
editor, Amy Clarke Moore.

pages cm

Includes index.

ISBN 978-1-62033-848-3

1. Knittng--Patterns. 2. Costume. 3. Wizards in
art. I. Moore, Amy Clarke.

TT825.K665 2014

746.43'2--dc23

201401110210

10 9 8 7 6 5 4 3 2 1

Introduction

These magical patterns were first published by Interweave in a publication that must not be named.

The designers who created these garments were inspired by worlds filled with fairies and elves, enchanted plants, talking mirrors, charmed handkerchiefs, witches and wizards, ghosts and giants, flying mortar and pestles, transformative combs, and heroic journeys out into the world and within oneself.

Fairy tales and mythology have intrigued writers and knitters alike for generations. While most of us were transfixed by these stories in our childhood, they provide a rich landscape for our imagination and roadmap for our adult lives as well.

In fairy tales and mythology, mundane objects such as handkerchiefs, cloaks, boots, and combs often become imbued with special properties that help a protagonist overcome obstacles and achieve feats once deemed impossible. As knitters, we have intimate knowledge of how ordinary tools and materials are given meaning and purpose: a garment made by hand is charged with love in every stitch.

This book is filled with inspired knitwear drawing on a love for literature and age-old stories from cultures around the world. We chose designs that subtly allude to our love of a hidden, magical life. We also wanted to create a balance between opposites—playful/serious; light/dark; inside/outside; wild/civilized; mundane/magic; hidden/visible; up/down; love/hate; tolerance/intolerance; good/evil.

We included designs that challenge the advanced knitter, engage the intermediate knitter, and invite the beginning knitter into this enchanted world of making something from nothing.

May your knitting be magical,

Amy Clarke Moore

May your words be sweet, May my

May your words be right,

Contents

ble fly fleet,

my future be bright.

Drop-Your-Guard Vest

❧ Emma Welford

This vest is a quirky take on a traditional layering piece. The body is worked in a multitextured stitch pattern that combines cables, eyelet lace, and dropped stitches when you get dreamy and distracted from memorizing new spells to cast. Knitted in one piece from the bottom up, the stitch pattern keeps you on your toes until the big reveal comes when select stitches are dropped at the end.

Finished Size
26½ (30½, 34, 38, 41½, 45½, 49)" (67.5 [77.5, 86.5, 96.5, 105.5, 124.5] cm) bust circumference, buttoned. Vest shown measures 30½" (77.5 cm).

Yarn
Imperial Yarn Columbia (100% wool; 220 yd [201 m]/4 oz [113 g]): #113 golden sun, 3 (4, 4, 4, 5, 5, 6) skeins.

Needles
Size 7 (4.5 mm): 32" circular (81.5 cm) (cir) and set of double-pointed (dpn). *Adjust needle size if necessary to obtain the correct gauge.*

Notions
Markers (m); stitch holders; cable needle (cn); tapestry needle; eight 1" (2.5 cm) buttons.

Gauge
20 sts and 28 rows = 4" (10 cm) in patt, after dropping sts.

Body

CO 132 (151, 170, 189, 208, 227, 246) sts. Do not join. Work in k1, p1 rib for 2" (5 cm), ending with a WS row. Purl 1 RS row. Work Cable and Lace chart for your size over all sts until piece measures 14" (35.5 cm) from CO, ending with a WS row.

Shape Armholes

Work 42 (48, 55, 60, 67, 73, 79) sts in patt, BO 4 (4, 4, 6, 6, 6, 6) sts for underarm (see Notes), work 62 (72, 81, 89, 98, 108, 117) sts for back, BO 4 (4, 4, 6, 6, 6, 6) sts for underarm, work to end—124 (143, 162, 177, 196, 215, 234) sts rem: 42 (48, 55, 60, 67, 73, 79) sts for right front, 62 (72, 81, 89, 98, 108, 117) sts for back, 20 (23, 26, 28, 31, 34, 38) sts for left front. Place right front and back sts on holders.

Left Front

Work 1 WS row. At beg of RS rows, BO 2 (2, 2, 3, 3, 3, 3) sts 2 times—16 (19, 22, 22, 25, 28, 32) sts rem. Work 1 WS row.

DEC ROW: (RS) K1, ssk, work to end—1 st dec'd. Rep Dec Row every 0 (6, 3, 2, 1, 1, 1) row(s) 0 (2, 4, 5, 8, 11, 13) more times, working WS Dec Row (if needed) as foll: Work to last 3 sts, ssp, p1—15 (16, 17, 16, 16, 16, 18) sts rem. Work even until armhole measures 3 (3, 3, 3½, 3½, 3¾, 3¾)" (7.5 [7.5, 7.5, 9, 9, 9.5, 9.5] cm), ending with a RS row.

Shape Neck

BO 1 (2, 3, 0, 0, 0, 2) st(s) at beg of next WS row—14 (14, 14, 16, 16, 16, 16) sts rem. Work even in patt until armhole measures 6¼ (6¾, 7¼, 7¾, 8¼, 8¾, 9¼)" (16 [17, 18.5, 19.5, 21, 22, 23.5] cm). Place sts on holder.

Back

With WS facing, rejoin yarn to 62 (72, 81, 89, 98, 108, 117) back sts.

Shape Armholes

BO 2 (2, 2, 3, 3, 3, 3) sts at beg of next 4 rows—54 (64, 73, 77, 86, 96, 105) sts rem. Work 1 WS row.

DEC ROW: (RS) K1, ssk, work to last 3 sts, k2tog, k1—2 sts dec'd. Rep Dec Row every 4 (2, 2, 1, 1, 1, 1) row(s) 1 (3, 4, 5, 7, 9, 11) more time(s), working WS Dec Row (if needed) as foll: P1, p2tog, work to last 3 sts, ssp, p1—50 (56, 63, 65, 70, 76, 81) sts rem. Work even in patt until armholes measure 4¼ (4¾, 5¼, 5¾, 6¼, 6¾, 7¼)" (11 [12, 13.5, 16, 17, 18.5] cm), ending with a WS row.

Shape Neck

Work 14 (14, 17, 18, 20, 22, 24) sts in patt, BO 22 (28, 29, 29, 30, 32, 33) sts, work to end—14 (14, 17, 18, 20, 22, 24) sts rem each side. Place right back sts on holder.

Left Back

Work 1 WS row. At beg of RS rows, BO 0 (0, 3, 2, 2, 3, 4) sts 0 (0, 1, 1, 2, 2, 2) time(s)—14 (14, 14, 16, 16, 16, 16) sts rem. Work even in patt until armhole measures 6¼ (6¾, 7¼, 7¾, 8¼, 8¾, 9¼)" (16 [17, 18.5, 19.5, 21, 22, 23.5] cm). Place sts on holder.

Right Back

With WS facing, rejoin yarn to right back shoulder. At beg of WS rows, BO 0 (0, 3, 2, 2, 3, 4) sts 0 (0, 1, 1, 2, 2, 2) time(s)—14 (14, 14, 16, 16, 16, 16) sts rem. Work even in patt until armhole measures 6¼ (6¾, 7¼, 7¾, 8¼, 8¾, 9¼)" (16 [17, 18.5, 19.5, 21, 22, 23.5] cm). Place sts on holder.

Right Front

With WS facing, rejoin yarn to 42 (48, 55, 60, 67, 73, 79) right front sts.

Shape Armhole

At beg of WS rows, BO 2 (2, 2, 3, 3, 3, 3) sts 2 times—38 (44, 51, 54, 61, 67, 73) sts rem.

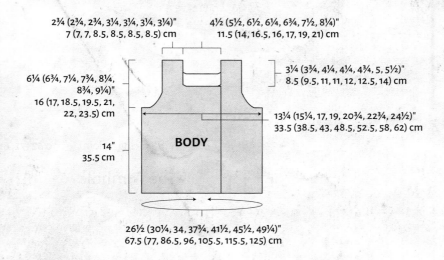

2¾ (2¾, 2¾, 3¼, 3¼, 3¼, 3¼)"
7 (7, 7, 8.5, 8.5, 8.5, 8.5) cm

4½ (5½, 6½, 6¼, 6¾, 7½, 8¼)"
11.5 (14, 16.5, 16, 17, 19, 21) cm

6¼ (6¾, 7¼, 7¾, 8¼, 8¾, 9¼)"
16 (17, 18.5, 19.5, 21, 22, 23.5) cm

3¼ (3¾, 4¼, 4¼, 4¾, 5, 5½)"
8.5 (9.5, 11, 11, 12, 12.5, 14) cm

13¼ (15¼, 17, 19, 20¾, 22¾, 24½)"
33.5 (38.5, 43, 48.5, 52.5, 58, 62) cm

BODY

14"
35.5 cm

26½ (30¼, 34, 37¾, 41½, 45½, 49¼)"
67.5 (77, 86.5, 96, 105.5, 115.5, 125) cm

DEC ROW: (RS) Work to last 3 sts, k2tog, k1—1 st dec'd. Rep Dec Row every 0 (6, 3, 2, 1, 1, 1) row(s) 0 (2, 4, 6, 9, 11, 13) more times, working WS Dec Row (if needed) as foll: P1, p2tog, work to end—37 (41, 46, 47, 51, 55, 59) sts rem. Work even until armhole measures 3 (3, 3, 3½, 3½, 3¾, 3¾)" (7.5 [7.5, 7.5, 9, 9, 9.5, 9.5] cm), ending with a WS row.

Shape Neck

BO 22 (25, 26, 28, 32, 35, 37) sts at beg of next RS row—15 (16, 20, 19, 19, 20, 22) sts rem. Work 1 WS row. At beg of RS rows, BO 1 (2, 3, 3, 3, 2, 3) st(s) 1 (1, 2, 1, 1, 2, 2) time(s)—14 (14, 14, 16, 16, 16, 16) sts rem. Work even until armhole measures 6¼ (6¾, 7¼, 7¾, 8¼, 8¾, 9¼)" (16 [17, 18.5, 19.5, 21, 22, 23.5] cm). Place sts on holder.

Finishing

With RS tog, join shoulders using three-needle BO (see Glossary).

Armband

With dpn and RS facing, pick up and knit 74 (80, 86, 92, 98, 104, 110) sts evenly spaced around armhole. Place marker (pm) and join in the rnd. Work in k1, p1 rib for 3 rnds. BO all sts in patt.

Neckband

With RS facing and beg at right front neck edge, pick up and knit 93 (107, 119, 117, 125, 137, 149) sts around neck opening, ending at left front neck edge. Do not join. Work in k1, p1 rib for 3 rows. With RS facing, BO all sts in patt.

Buttonband

With RS facing, pick up and knit 81 (81, 81, 83, 83, 85, 85) sts along left front edge. Work in k1, p1 rib for 9 rows. With RS facing, BO all sts in patt. Mark for placement of 8 buttons, one 1" (2.5 cm) from lower edge, one 1" (2.5 cm) from neck edge, and others evenly spaced between.

Buttonhole Band

With RS facing, pick up and knit 81 (81, 81, 83, 83, 85, 85) sts along right front edge. Work in k1, p1 rib for 3 rows.

BUTTONHOLE ROW: (RS) Cont in patt, work 2-st one-row buttonhole (see Glossary) opposite each m. Work 5 rows even, ending with a WS row. With RS facing, BO all sts in patt. Weave in loose ends. Block to measurements. 🦉

EMMA WELFORD designs dreamy knitwear and harasses her cats in Greenfield, Massachusetts. You can find her online at emmawelford.com.

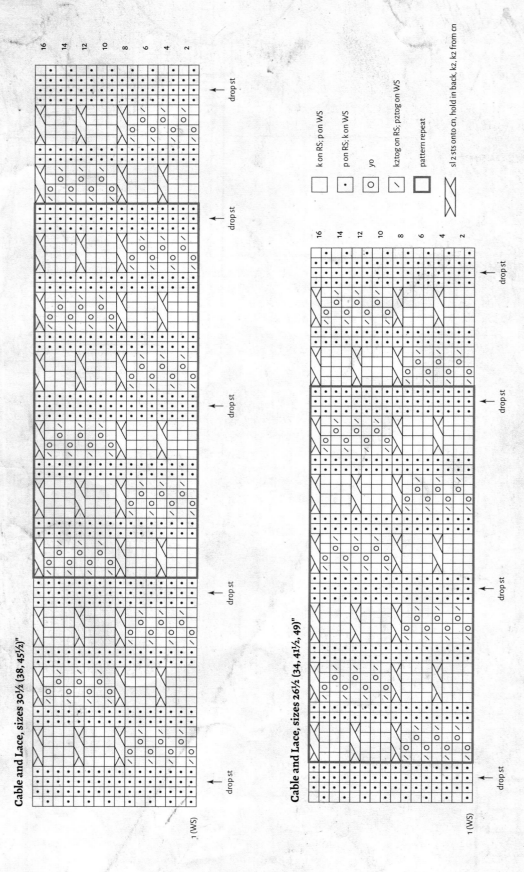

Cable and Lace, sizes 30½ (38, 45½)"

Cable and Lace, sizes 26½ (34, 41½, 49)"

Legend:
- k on RS; p on WS
- p on RS; k on WS
- yo
- k2tog on RS; p2tog on WS
- pattern repeat
- sl 2 sts onto cn, hold in back, k2, k2 from cn

Sorcery Sweater

⁂ Catherine Salter Bayar

Celtic knotwork provides the inspiration for this masculine wool sweater. A budding sorcerer will certainly love the baroque details inspired by ornate crosses and highly textured carving. Brawny cables and fluid I-cord motifs stand out against a horizontal rib ground in mossy green.

Finished Size

39 (43¼, 47¾)" (99 [110, 121.5] cm) chest circumference. Sweater shown measures 43¼" (110 cm).

Yarn

Cascade Yarns Cascade 220 Sport (100% Peruvian Highland wool; 164 yd [150 m]/1¾ oz [50 g]): #9448 olive heather, 11 (12, 13) skeins.

Needles

Size 4 (3.5 mm): 16" (40.5 cm) and 29" (73.5 cm) circular (cir); size 6 (4 mm): 29" (73.5 cm) cir and set of double-pointed (dpn); size 7 (4.5 mm). *Adjust needle size if necessary to obtain the correct gauge.*

Notions

Markers (m); stitch holders; cable needle (cn); straight pins; tapestry needle.

Gauge

22 sts and 34 rnds = 4" (10 cm) in rev St st on middle-size needle; 38 (42, 46) sts of Cable chart = 5¼ (6, 6¾)" (13.5 [15, 17] cm) wide on middle-size needle.

NOTES

❋ *Charts for sizes 39 and 47¾ can be found online at knittingdaily.com.*

❋ *The body is worked in one piece from the bottom in the round to the armholes, then front and back are worked separately.*

❋ *I-cord trims in various lengths are applied through openings and along guidelines worked in while knitting the chest.*

Body

With smallest needle, CO 228 (252, 276) sts. Place marker (pm) and join in the rnd. Work in k2, p2 rib for 1½" (3.8 cm). Change to middle-size needle. Work Rows 1–16 of Cable chart for your size 4 times.

NEXT RND: Work Row 1 of Front chart for your size over 114 (126, 138) sts, pm, work 5 (7, 9) sts in patt, pm for waist shaping, work in cable patt to last 5 (7, 9) sts, pm for waist shaping, work to end. Work 1 rnd even.

INC RND: Work in patt to 2nd m, M1P, sl m, work in patt to m, sl m, M1P, work to end—4 sts inc'd. Rep Inc Rnd every 4th rnd 9 more times—268 (292, 316) sts. Work even through Row 50 of chart, ending 4 sts before end of rnd on last rnd.

NEXT RND: BO 4 sts, work Row 51 of Front chart, BO 4 sts of back, work to end—126 (138, 150) sts rem for each of front and back. Place front sts on holder.

Back

Work 1 WS row. BO 2 sts at beg of next 2 rows—122 (134, 146) sts rem.

KNIT DEC ROW: (RS) Ssk, work to last 2 sts, k2tog—2 sts dec'd. Work 1 WS row.

PURL DEC ROW: (RS) Ssp, work to last 2 sts, p2tog—2 sts dec'd. Work 1 WS row.

Rep last 4 rows 2 more times, then work Knit Dec Row once more—108 (120, 132) sts rem.

Work through Row 16 of Cable chart, then work Rows 1–16 two more times, then work Rows 1–12 once more—11 cable crosses from CO.

Shape Neck

NEXT ROW: (RS; Row 13 of chart) Work 42 (48, 54) sts in patt, BO 24 sts for neck, work in patt to end—42 (48, 54) sts rem each side. Place right back sts on holder.

Left Back

Work 1 WS row. At beg of RS rows, BO 4 (5, 6) sts once, then BO 5 sts once, then BO 2 sts once—31 (36, 41) sts rem. Work 1 WS row. BO all sts.

Right Back

With WS facing, rejoin yarn to right back sts. At beg of WS rows, BO 4 (5, 6) sts once, then BO 5 sts once, then BO 2 sts once—31 (36, 41) sts rem. Work 2 rows even. BO all sts.

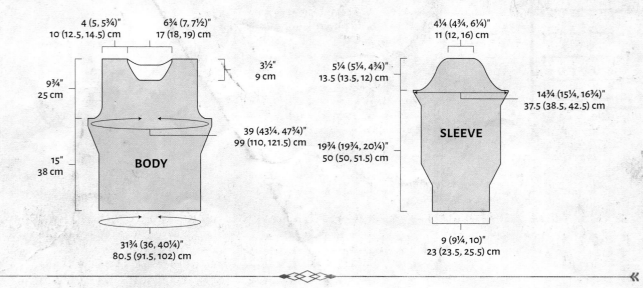

BODY

4 (5, 5¾)"
10 (12.5, 14.5) cm

6¾ (7, 7½)"
17 (18, 19) cm

3½"
9 cm

9¾"
25 cm

39 (43¼, 47¾)"
99 (110, 121.5) cm

15"
38 cm

31¾ (36, 40¼)"
80.5 (91.5, 102) cm

SLEEVE

4¼ (4¾, 6¼)"
11 (12, 16) cm

5¼ (5¼, 4¾)"
13.5 (13.5, 12) cm

14¾ (15¼, 16¾)"
37.5 (38.5, 42.5) cm

19¾ (19¾, 20¼)"
50 (50, 51.5) cm

9 (9¼, 10)"
23 (23.5, 25.5) cm

Front

With WS facing, rejoin yarn to 126 (138, 150) front sts. Work Rows 52–102 of Front chart—108 (120, 132) sts rem.

NEXT ROW: (RS; Row 103 of chart) Work 42 (47, 52) sts in patt, BO 24 (26, 28) sts as shown on chart, work in patt to end—42 (47, 52) sts rem for each front. Place left front sts on holder.

Right Front

Work through Row 132 of chart—31 (36, 41) sts rem. BO all sts.

Left Front

With WS facing, rejoin yarn to 42 (47, 52) left front sts. Work Rows 104–132 of chart—31 (36, 41) sts rem. BO all sts.

Sleeves

With smallest needle, CO 58 (60, 64) sts. Do not join. Work in k2, p2 rib for 2¼" (5.5 cm), ending with a RS row. Change to middle-size needle:

SET-UP ROW: (WS) P17 (18, 20), k2, p20, k2, p17 (18, 20). Work Rows 1–16 of Sleeve chart for your size once.

Shape Sleeve

Cont in patt, inc 1 st each end of needle on next row, then every 4th row 7 (7, 8) more times, working new sts into welt patt—74 (76, 82) sts. Change to largest needles. Work even through Row 16 of chart, then work Rows 1–16 of chart 4 (4, 3) more times—7 cable crosses from CO. Inc 1 st each end of needle on next row, then every 4th row 4 (4, 5) more times—84 (86, 94) sts. Work 1 WS row.

Shape Cap

BO 5 sts at beg of next 2 rows, then BO 3 sts at beg of foll 2 rows, then BO 2 sts at beg of foll 6 rows—56 (58, 66) sts rem; Row 12 (12, 16) of chart is complete. Work 12 (12, 8) rows even, ending with Row 8 of chart. Dec 1 st each end of needle every RS row 4 times, then every row 8 times—32 (34, 42) sts rem. Loosely BO all sts.

Finishing

I-Cords

With middle-size dpn and holding 2 strands tog, work 4-st I-cords (see Glossary) in foll lengths: Center circle, 12" (30.5 cm); center horizontal with 2 overhand knots, 28 (30, 32)" (71 [76, 81.5] cm); top, 2 I-cords, each 9 (10, 11)" (23 [25.5, 28] cm); bottom, 2 I-cords, each 12 (13, 14)" (30.5 [33, 35.5] cm); middle with 1 overhand knot, 2 I-cords, each 15 (16, 17)" (38 [40.5, 43] cm).

Place I-cords

Note: *St st rows across chest are guidelines for placing I-cords. In foll instructions, "left" and "right" refer to garment as you are looking at it.*

Center

Insert center circle I-cord through top right and bottom left openings in center cable patt, tucking ends to WS and forming a circle. Tie a loose overhand knot about 7 (7½, 8)" (18 [19, 20.5] cm) from end of center horizontal I-cord. Insert short end through top left opening in center cable patt, using a straight pin to secure end on WS in center behind cable. With I-cord going over center circle, pin overhand knot over left chest where center guidelines end. Work long end of I-cord under center circle, over cable, through bottom right opening, and over center circle. Loosely tie a 2nd overhand knot and pin over right chest where center guidelines end. Work rem end under center circle, over cable, and into top left opening. Pin ends of I-cord tog on WS. Checking to see that center circle and center horizontal I-cords are as shown in photo, sew I-cords to body, sewing along underside of I-cord with yarn and tapestry needle.

Top

Coil end of I-cord and place in area between center cable and point at base of welts, then pin rest of length horizontally to armhole. Sew in place.

Bottom

Coil end of I-cord and place in area between center cable and point at top of welts, then pin rest of length horizontally to underarm. Sew in place.

Middle

Loosely tie an overhand knot at center of I-cord. Pin one end of I-cord over bottom knitted guideline. Adjust knot and place at end of guideline, leaving about a 1" (2.5 cm) gap between it and center knotted I-cord. Pin rem end over top guideline, crossing ends as shown in photo. Sew in place.

Cable, size 43¼"

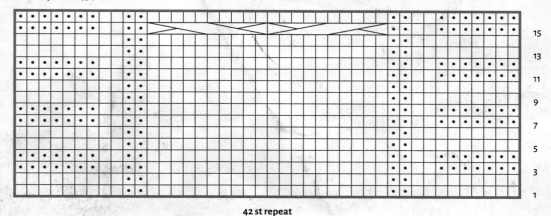

42 st repeat

Sleeve, size 43¼"

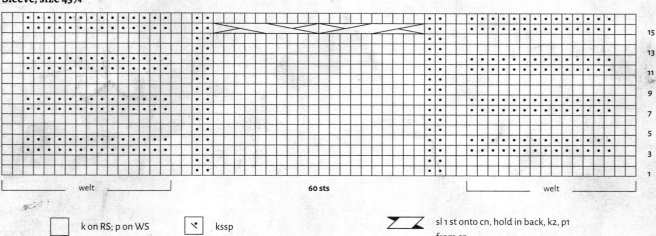

welt   60 sts   welt

▢ k on RS; p on WS	↘ kssp	sl 1 st onto cn, hold in back, k2, p1 from cn
• p on RS; k on WS	MP M1P	sl 2 sts onto cn, hold in front, p1, k2 from cn
╱ k2tog	⌒ bind off 1 st	sl 5 sts onto cn, hold in back, k5, k5 from cn
╲ ssk	▢ pattern repeat	sl 5 sts onto cn, hold in front, k5, k5 from cn
↗ p2tog		

Neck Rib

With smallest 16" (40.5 cm) cir needle, pick up and knit 152 (156, 164) sts evenly spaced around neck opening. Pm and join in the rnd. Work in k2, p2 rib for 1" (2.5 cm). Loosely BO all sts. Sew sleeve seams. Sew in sleeves. Weave in loose ends. Very lightly block garment without flattening texture of rib, cables, and I-cords. 🕸

California native **CATHERINE SALTER BAYAR** is a clothing, interior, and knitwear designer who relocated to Turkey in 1999 to pursue her love of handmade textiles and fiber arts. Bazaar Bayar is a handcrafts workshop she founded in Istanbul to provide work for local artisans and to teach visiting women about Turkish handcrafts both traditional and modern. Learn more at bazaarbayar.com.

Front, size 43¼" (lower left)

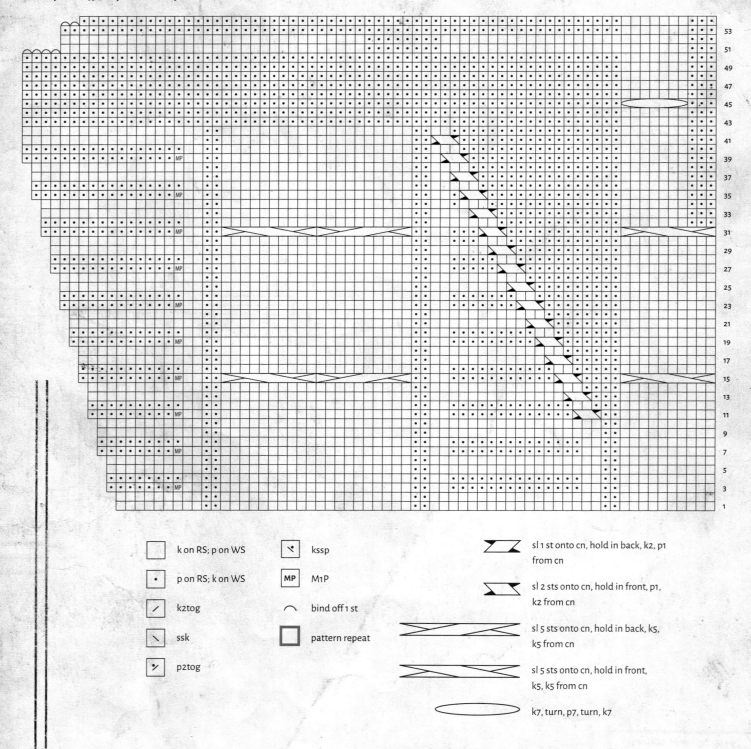

	k on RS; p on WS		kssp		sl 1 st onto cn, hold in back, k2, p1 from cn
•	p on RS; k on WS	**MP**	M1P		sl 2 sts onto cn, hold in front, p1, k2 from cn
/	k2tog	⌒	bind off 1 st		sl 5 sts onto cn, hold in back, k5, k5 from cn
\	ssk		pattern repeat		sl 5 sts onto cn, hold in front, k5, k5 from cn
⌐	p2tog			⬭	k7, turn, p7, turn, k7

Front, size 43¼" (lower right)

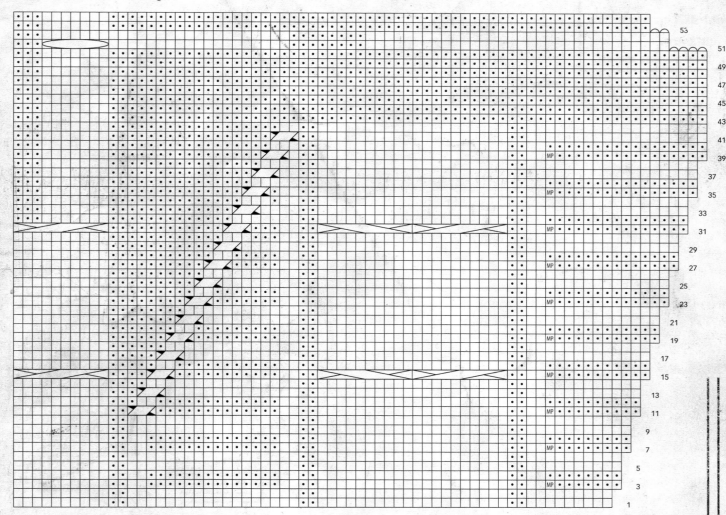

Front, size 43¼" (upper left)

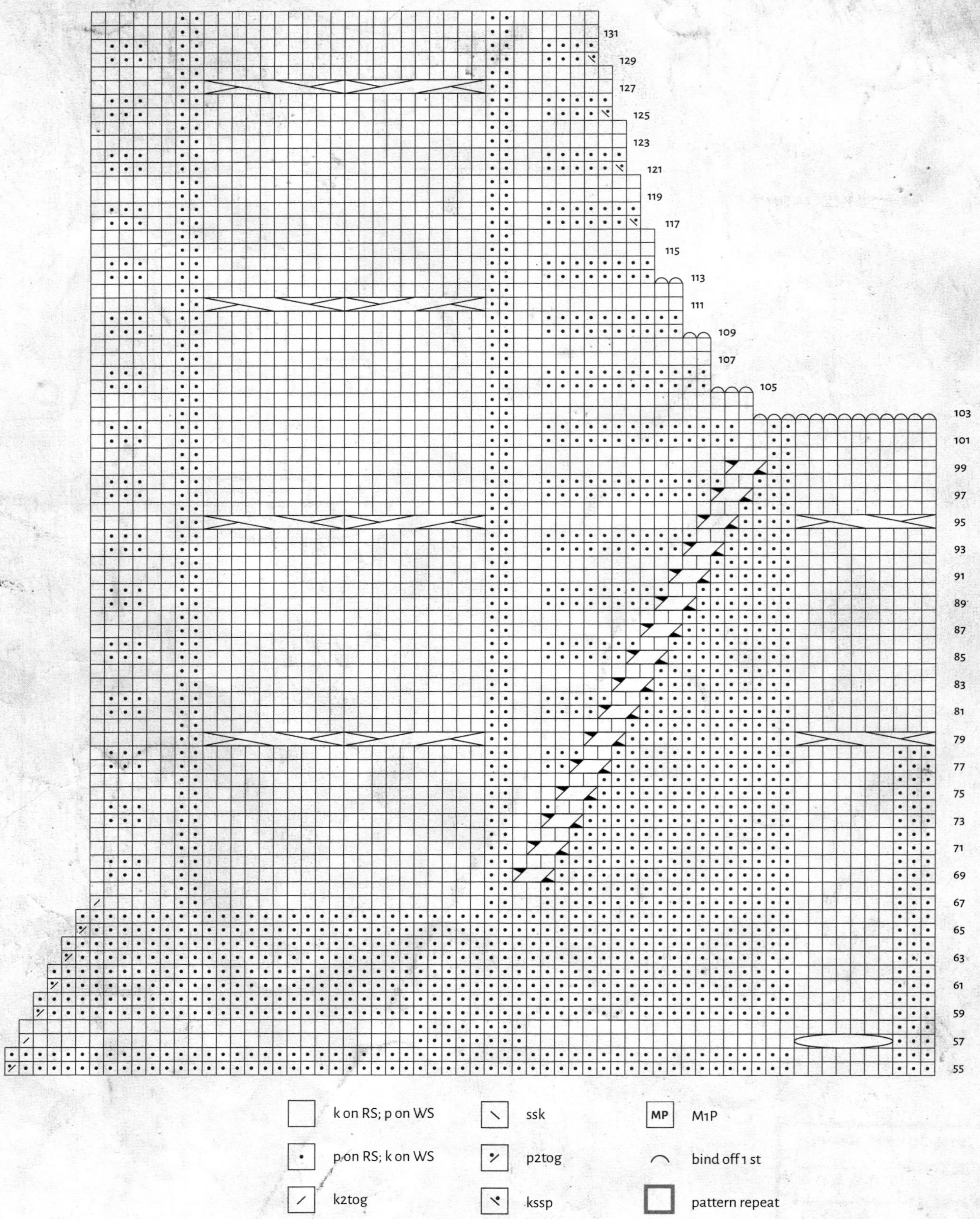

Row numbers (right side, top to bottom): 131, 129, 127, 125, 123, 121, 119, 117, 115, 113, 111, 109, 107, 105, 103, 101, 99, 97, 95, 93, 91, 89, 87, 85, 83, 81, 79, 77, 75, 73, 71, 69, 67, 65, 63, 61, 59, 57, 55

Symbol	Meaning
□	k on RS; p on WS
•	p on RS; k on WS
/	k2tog
\	ssk
p2tog symbol	p2tog
kssp symbol	kssp
MP	M1P
⌢	bind off 1 st
□	pattern repeat

Front, size 43¼" (upper right)

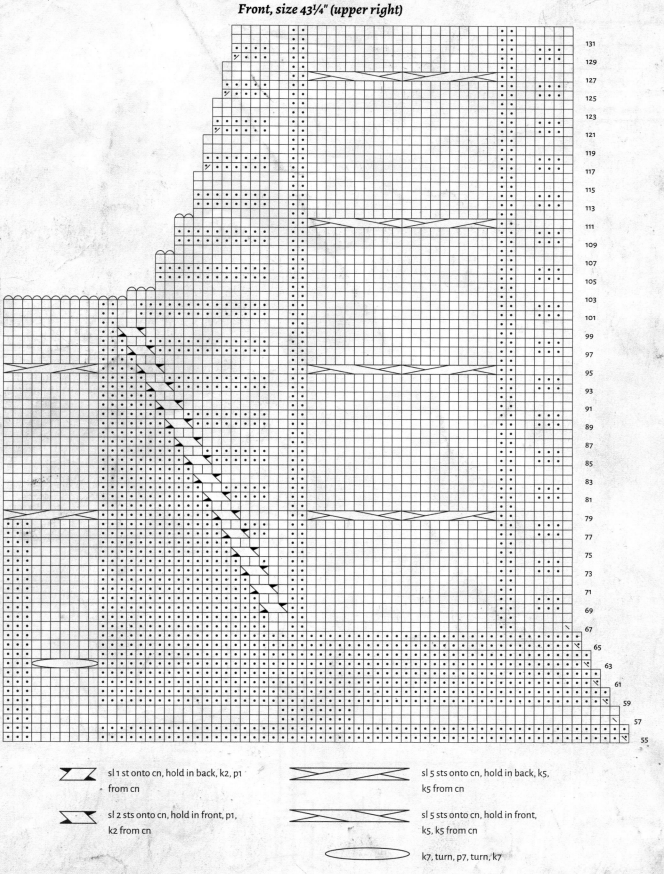

131
129
127
125
123
121
119
117
115
113
111
109
107
105
103
101
99
97
95
93
91
89
87
85
83
81
79
77
75
73
71
69
67
65
63
61
59
57
55

sl 1 st onto cn, hold in back, k2, p1 from cn

sl 2 sts onto cn, hold in front, p1, k2 from cn

sl 5 sts onto cn, hold in back, k5, k5 from cn

sl 5 sts onto cn, hold in front, k5, k5 from cn

k7, turn, p7, turn, k7

Griffin Socks

⸎ Anne Podlesak

These unisex socks are knitted from the cuff down, featuring a standard square heel flap and a wide tapered toe. The different stitch patterns side by side call to mind the wings and talons of the mythical griffin, a creature that is part eagle, part lion.

Finished Size

Men's 8½ (9, 10)" (21.5 [23, 25.5] cm) foot circumference, 10 (10, 10¼)" foot length from back of heel to tip of toe. Shown in 9" (23 cm) circumference.

Yarn

Wooly Wonka Fibers Ceridwen Sock (100% superwash Merino; 400 yd [366 m]/3½ oz [100 g]): brocade, 1 (2, 2) skein(s).

Needles

1 (2.25 mm): set of 5 double-pointed (dpn). *Adjust needle size if necessary to obtain the correct gauge.*

Notions

Markers (m); cable needle (cn); stitch holder; tapestry needle.

Gauge

34 sts and 50 rows = 4" (10 cm) in St st.

Sock

Leg

CO 72 (76, 84) sts. Divide evenly onto 4 dpn. Place marker (pm) and join in the rnd. Work in k1, p1 rib for 1" (2.5 cm). Work Rows 1–21 (25, 23) of Griffin chart for your size. Work in k1, p1 rib for 1" (2.5 cm). Work Rows 1–24 of Gargoyle chart for your size 2 (2, 3) times, then work Row 1 once more.

Heel Flap

Place last 36 (38, 42) sts on holder for instep. Work heel back and forth in rows on rem 36 (38, 42) sts.

NEXT ROW: (RS) *Sl 1 pwise with yarn in front (wyf), k1; rep from * to end.

NEXT ROW: (WS) Sl 1 pwise with yarn in back (wyb), purl to end.

Rep last 2 rows 17 (18, 20) more times—36 (38, 42) rows completed.

Turn Heel

SHORT-ROW 1: (RS) K21 (22, 24), ssk, k1, turn.

SHORT-ROW 2: (WS) Sl 1 pwise wyf, p7, p2tog, p1, turn.

SHORT-ROW 3: (RS) Sl 1 pwise wyb, knit to 1 st before gap, ssk, k1, turn.

SHORT-ROW 4: (WS) Sl 1 pwise wyf, purl to 1 st before gap, p2tog, p1, turn.

Rep last 2 short-rows 6 (6, 7) more times—20 (22, 24) sts rem.

Gusset

NEXT RND: (RS) On needle 1, K20 (22, 24) heel sts, pick up and knit 18 (19, 21) sts along the edge of the heel flap; on needles 2 and 3, beg with Row 2 of Gargoyle chart, work across 36 (38, 42) instep sts in patt as established; on needle 4, pick up and knit 18 (19, 21) sts along the edge of the heel flap, k10 (11, 12) heel sts from needle 1 to needle 4—92 (98, 108) sts total. Pm for new beg of rnd (at the center of the heel). Needles 1 and 4 are the sole of the foot sts and will be worked in St st. Needles 2 and 3 are the instep and will be worked in the Gargoyle chart patt.

DEC RND: Knit to the last 3 sts on needle 1, k2tog, k1; cont even in patt across needles 2 and 3; on needle 4, k1, ssk, knit to end—2 sts dec'd.

Work 1 rnd even in patt.

Rep last 2 rnds 9 (10, 11) more times—72 (76, 84) sts rem.

Foot

Work even in patt as established until the foot measures about 8" from the back of the heel, ending with Row 24 of the Gargoyle chart. Work 4 more rnds, maintaining St st on the sole of the foot, and working Row 25 of the Gargoyle chart on the top of the foot.

Note: *Sock will measure about 2 (2, 2¼)" less than total desired foot length.*

Toe

DEC RND: Knit to the last 3 sts on needle 1, k2tog, k1; on needle 2, k1, ssk, and knit to the end; on needle 3, knit to the last 3 sts, k2tog, k1; on needle 4, k1, ssk, knit to end—4 sts dec'd.

Knit 1 rnd even.

Rep last 2 rnds 12 (12, 14) more times—20 (24, 24) sts rem. Knit sts from needle 1 onto needle 4. Then sl sts from needles 2 and 3 onto 1 needle. Break yarn, leaving a long tail for grafting.

Finishing

With tail threaded on a tapestry needle, graft sts using Kitchener st (see Glossary). Weave in ends. 🦁

ANNE PODLESAK of White Rock, New Mexico, has been knitting since the squirmy age of six. She was taught to knit by her grandmother and great-aunt in an attempt to get her to sit still but didn't officially become an addict until she was in high school, at which point, there was no looking back. She is the owner of the indie dye studio Wooly Wonka Fibers.

Gargoyle, size 8½"

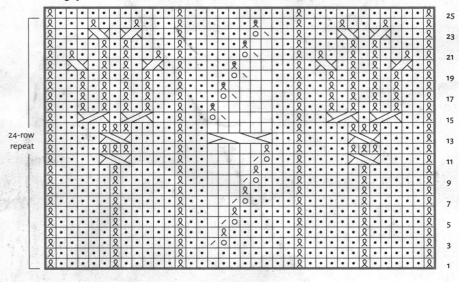

24-row repeat

36 st repeat

Gargoyle, size 9"

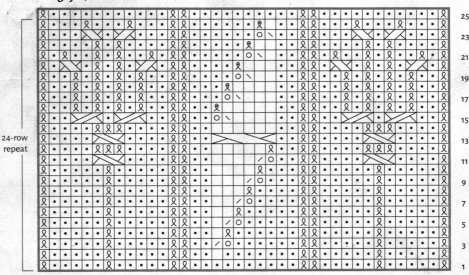

24-row repeat

38 st repeat

☐	knit	
•	purl	
o	yo	
/	k2tog	
\	ssk	

Ω	k1tbl	
Ƣ	p1tbl	
☐	pattern repeat	

B — MB: [K1, yo, k1, yo, k1] into next st, turn. K5, turn. P5, turn. K2tog, k1, k2tog, turn. P3tog.

sl 1 st onto cn, hold in back, k1, k1 from cn

sl 1 st onto cn, hold in front, k1, k1 from cn

sl 2 sts onto cn, hold in back, k1, k2 from cn

sl 1 st onto cn, hold in front, k2, k1 from cn

sl 3 sts onto cn, hold in front, k3, k3 from cn

Gargoyle, size 10"

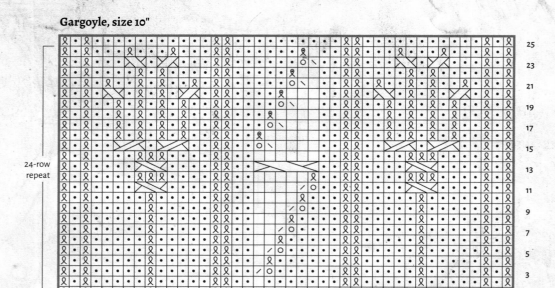

24-row repeat

25
23
21
19
17
15
13
11
9
7
5
3
1

42 st repeat

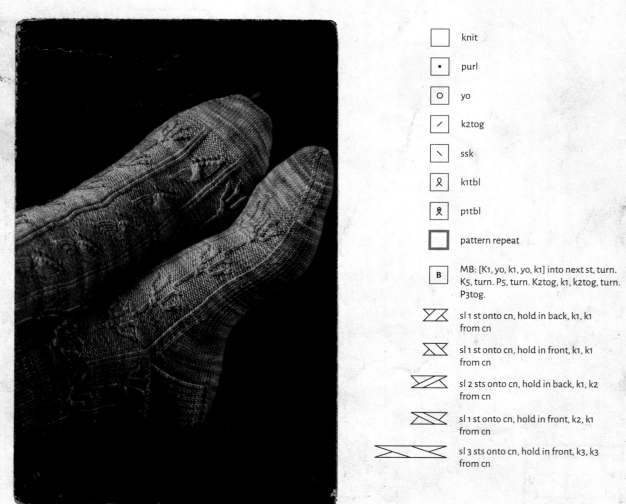

	knit
•	purl
O	yo
/	k2tog
\	ssk
ʊ	k1tbl
ᶇ	p1tbl
☐	pattern repeat
B	MB: [K1, yo, k1, yo, k1] into next st, turn. K5, turn. P5, turn. K2tog, k1, k2tog, turn. P3tog.

sl 1 st onto cn, hold in back, k1, k1 from cn

sl 1 st onto cn, hold in front, k1, k1 from cn

sl 2 sts onto cn, hold in back, k1, k2 from cn

sl 1 st onto cn, hold in front, k2, k1 from cn

sl 3 sts onto cn, hold in front, k3, k3 from cn

Griffin, size 8½"

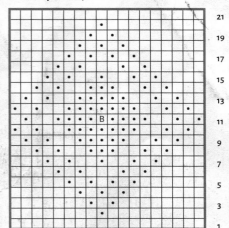

18 st repeat

Griffin, size 9"

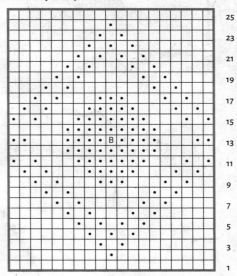

19 st repeat

Griffin, size 10"

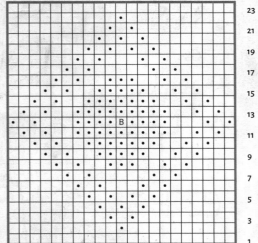

21 st repeat

	knit
•	purl
B	MB: [K1, yo, k1, yo, k1] into next st, turn. K5, turn. P5, turn. K2tog, k1, k2tog, turn. P3tog.

Tracery Vest

⊹ Kathleen Sperling

This garment was inspired by Gothic-style stained-glass windows, such as those found in castles defended against dragons. The name of the pattern, Tracery, is the term used for the stonework sections that contain the glass of Gothic windows.

Finished Size
30¾(35, 38¾, 43, 46¾, 52)" (78 [89, 98.5, 109, 118.5, 132] cm) bust circumference with 2¾ (3, 2¾, 3, 2¾, 4)" (7 [7.5, 7, 7.5, 7, 10] cm) positive ease. Vest shown measures 35" (89 cm).

Yarn
Plymouth Yarn Company Happy Feet (90% Merino, 10% nylon; 192 yd [176 m]/1¾ oz [50 g]): #500 (MC), 3 (3, 3, 3, 4, 4) skeins; #27 (CC), 2 (2, 3, 3, 3, 3) skeins.

Needles
Size 2.5 (3 mm): 16" (40.5 cm) and 24–32" (61–81.5 cm) circular (cir). *Adjust needle size if necessary to obtain the correct gauge.*

Notions
Markers (m); cable needle (cn); stitch holder; tapestry needle.

Gauge
30 sts and 33 rows = 4" (10 cm) in chart patt st, blocked.

Stitch Guide

2-color rib (multiple of 4 sts)

RND 1: *With MC, k2, with CC, p2; rep from * to end. Rep Rnd 1 for patt.

NOTES

✻ *When working in the round, read all chart rows from right to left.*

✻ *When working back and forth in rows, read RS chart rows from right to left and WS rows from left to right.*

✻ *When increasing, incorporate the new sts into the chart patt.*

✻ *Make any decreases or bind-offs in chart patt, unless otherwise indicated.*

Body

With MC, longer needle and long-tail method (see Glossary), CO 200 (224, 252, 280, 312, 340) sts.

Place marker (pm) and join in the rnd. Join CC and work in 2-color rib (see Stitch Guide) for 5¾" (14.5 cm). With MC, knit 1 rnd. Purl 1 rnd.

NEXT RND: With MC, purl inc 2 sts evenly around—202 (226, 254, 282, 314, 342) sts.

SET-UP RND: [With MC, k1, beg and ending as indicated for your size, work Tracery chart over 99 (111, 125, 139, 155, 169) sts, with MC, k1, pm] 2 times (using rnd m as last pm).

INC RND: [With MC, k1, LLI, work in patt to 1 st before m, RLI, with MC, k1, sl m] 2 times—4 sts inc'd. Rep Inc Rnd every other rnd 6

(8, 8, 9, 8, 11) more times—230 (262, 290, 322, 350, 390) sts. Work even in patt until piece measures 9" (23 cm) from CO edge.

Divide for Front and Back

Place last 115 (131, 145, 161, 175, 195) sts on holder for back.

Front

BO 7 (9, 10, 10, 11, 14) sts at beg of next 2 rows, then BO 3 (5, 5, 5, 6, 6) sts at beg of next 2 (2, 2, 4, 4, 4) rows, then BO 0 (0, 0, 0, 2, 3) sts at beg of next 0 (0, 0, 0, 2, 2) rows—95 (103, 115, 121, 125, 137) sts rem. Dec 1 st at each end of every RS row 4 (6, 6, 3, 2, 3) times—87 (91, 103, 115, 121, 131) sts rem. Work 3 (1, 1, 1, 1, 1) more row(s) even in patt, ending with a WS row.

NEXT ROW: (RS) Ssk 0 (1, 1, 1, 1, 1) time(s), work in patt across next 43 (43, 49, 55, 58, 63) sts, join new yarn and BO 1 st, work in patt to last 0 (2, 2, 2, 2, 2) sts, k2tog 0 (1, 1, 1, 1, 1) time(s)—86 (88, 100, 112, 118, 128) sts rem; 43 (44, 50, 56, 59, 64) sts each side.

Sizes 30¾ (35, 38¾)" only

Working each side separately, dec 1 st at each neck edge every RS row 27 (28, 29) times—16 (16, 21) sts rem each side. Armhole measures 8½ (9, 9¼)" (21.5 [23, 23.5] cm). Break yarn and place all rem sts on holder.

Sizes 43 (46¾, 52)" only

Working each side separately, dec 1 st at each end of every RS row 3 (5, 8) times, then dec 1 st at each neck edge every RS row 29 (28, 25) times—21 (21, 23) sts rem. Armhole measures 9½ (9¾, 10)" (24 [25, 25.5] cm). Break yarn and place all rem sts on holder.

Back

With RS facing, place 115 (131, 145, 161, 175, 195) back sts from holder onto needle. Join yarns as needed. BO 7 (9, 10, 10, 11, 14) sts at beg of next 2 rows, then BO 3 (5, 5, 5, 6, 6) sts at beg of next 2 (2, 2, 4, 4, 4) rows, then BO 0 (0, 0, 0, 2, 3) sts at beg of next 0 (0, 0, 0, 2, 2) rows—95 (103, 115, 121, 125, 137) sts rem. Dec 1 st at each end of every RS row 4 (7, 7, 7, 8, 12) times—87 (89, 101, 107, 109, 113) sts rem. Work even in patt until armhole measures 8½ (9, 9¼, 9½, 9¾, 10)" (21.5 [23, 23.5, 24, 25, 25.5] cm), ending with same chart row as front. Break yarns, leaving sts on needle.

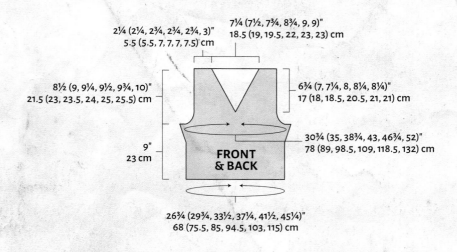

2¼ (2¼, 2¾, 2¾, 2¾, 3)"
5.5 (5.5, 7, 7, 7, 7.5) cm

7¼ (7½, 7¾, 8¾, 9, 9)"
18.5 (19, 19.5, 22, 23, 23) cm

8½ (9, 9¼, 9½, 9¾, 10)"
21.5 (23, 23.5, 24, 25, 25.5) cm

6¾ (7, 7¼, 8, 8¼, 8¼)"
17 (18, 18.5, 20.5, 21, 21) cm

30¾ (35, 38¾, 43, 46¾, 52)"
78 (89, 98.5, 109, 118.5, 132) cm

FRONT & BACK

9"
23 cm

26¾ (29¾, 33½, 37¼, 41½, 45¼)"
68 (75.5, 85, 94.5, 103, 115) cm

Finishing
Join Back and Front

With RS facing, place first 16 (16, 21, 21, 21, 23) sts of right back shoulder sts on holder, place next 55 (57, 59, 65, 67, 67) center back sts on waste yarn—16 (16, 21, 21, 21, 23) left back shoulder sts rem on needle.

Join Shoulders

Place 16 (16, 21, 21, 21, 23) left front shoulder sts from holder onto shorter needle. With MC, join front and back shoulders using three-needle BO (see Glossary). Rep for right shoulder.

Neck Edging

With RS facing, place the 55 (57, 59, 65, 67, 67) center back sts from waste yarn onto shorter needle.

NEXT RND: With MC, pick up 1 st in the gap between the right front neck edge and the center back sts and knit it tog with the first center back st, k53 (55, 57, 63, 65, 65), sl 1, pick up 1 st in the gap between the center back sts and left front neck edge, sl st back to left needle and k2tog, pick up and knit 52 (55, 58, 63, 66, 66) sts evenly along left front neck edge, pick up and knit 1

st at center bottom of neck, pick up and knit 52 (55, 58, 63, 66, 66) sts evenly along right front neck edge—160 (168, 176, 192, 200, 200) sts. Pm and join in rnd. Work 5 rnds in 2-color rib. With MC, BO all sts in patt.

Armhole Edgings

With RS facing, MC, and beg at bottom of armhole, pick up and knit 10 (14, 15, 20, 25, 29) sts along the BO edges of one side of armhole, pick up and knit 59 (63, 64, 65, 64, 66) sts up one edge of armhole, pick up and knit 1 st at top of armhole, pick up and knit 59 (63, 64, 65, 64, 66) sts down the other edge of armhole, pick up and knit 10 (14, 15, 20, 25, 29) sts along the BO edges of the other side of armhole, pick up and knit 1 st at center bottom of armhole—140 (156, 160, 172, 180, 192) sts. Pm and join in rnd. Work 5 rnds in 2-color rib. With MC, BO all sts in patt. Weave in all ends. Block to measurements.

KATHLEEN SPERLING learned how to knit when she was about seven, but became utterly obsessed with it in adulthood, trying out any technique that struck her fancy, no matter how simple or complex. Eventually, she began thinking up her own patterns and now finds herself spontaneously inspired with ideas. This, naturally, has led to an extremely large list of works in progress, which are chronicled at wipinsanity.blogspot.com.

Tracery

Thinking Cap

⚜ Moira Engel

$\mathcal{A}$ ny wizard worth his or her salt needs a colorful cap to help contain the abundance of percolating ideas. On the top of the hat, anything from pom-poms to tassels could be used to make a creative and individual statement. The piece is knitted in the round, so no sewing! It also uses an I-cord cast-on and bind-off to define the architecture. I-cord is wonderful to use in place of ribbing to give stockinette stitch support and prevent rolling edges.

Finished Size

20¾ (22, 23¼)" (52.5 [56, 59] cm) circumference and 8¾ (9, 9¼)" (22 [23, 23.5] cm) tall. Hat shown measures 22" (56 cm).

Yarn

Berroco Ultra Alpaca Light (50% superfine alpaca, 50% Peruvian wool; 144 yd [133 m]/1¾ oz [50 g]): #4284 prune mix (A), #4282 boysenberry mix (B), #4285 oceanic mix (C), #4288 blueberry mix (D), 1 skein each.

Needles

Size 6 (4 mm): set of 5 double-pointed (dpn); optional size 6 (4 mm) circular (cir). *Adjust needle size if necessary to obtain the correct gauge.*

Notions

Markers (m); tapestry needle; (optional) glass "e" 6/0 beads.

Gauge

23 sts and 28 rows = 4" (10 cm) in St st.

Hat

With A, CO 6 sts. Work 6-st I-cord (see Glossary) for 20¾ (22, 23¼)" (52.5 [56, 59] cm). BO all sts. With RS facing and A, pick up and knit 119 (126, 133) sts along edge of I-cord, being careful not to twist cord. Place marker (pm) and join to work in the rnd. Knit 1 rnd. Ending as indicated for your size, work Rnds 1–21 of Fair Isle chart. With A, work in St st until piece measures 5¼ (5½, 5¾)" (13.5 [14, 14.5] cm) from bottom of I-cord edge. Work 3-st I-cord BO (see Glossary) over all sts—3 sts rem. BO rem sts as foll: Sl 1, k2tog, psso—1 st rem. Do not break yarn.

Crown

With RS facing, pick up and knit 109 (119, 129) sts from I-cord BO edge—110 (120, 130) sts, including st rem on needle from I-cord BO. Pm and join in the rnd. Knit 1 rnd.

NEXT RND: [K10, pm] 11 (12, 13) times (using rnd m as last pm).

DEC RND: [Knit to 2 sts before m, ktog, sl m] 11 (12, 13) times—11 (12, 13) sts dec'd. Knit 2 rnds even. Rep last 3 rnds 7 more times—22 (24, 26) sts rem.

NEXT RND: [K2tog] 11 (12, 13) times—11 (12, 13) sts rem. Break yarn and thread through rem sts. Pull tight to close.

Finishing

Graft 6-st I-cord edges tog. Weave in ends.

Tassels

Cut 6 lengths of 32" (81.5 cm) yarn choosing any combination from the 4 yarn colors. With a tapestry needle, sl the lengths of yarn through the top knot of the hat so that 6 strands of 16" (40.5 cm) are on either side of the top knot. Arrange the yarn strands in 3 groups of 4, using pieces from both sides. Braid for 5" (12.5 cm) and then make a knot, leaving the ends free. Add beads to 1 or 2 (or more) strands for a snazzier tassel. ❦

MOIRA ENGEL is a Pacific Northwest designer married to a tugboat captain. Comfort requires a certain creativity with warm woolies for wet weather. Moira desires to design unique items that are fun to knit and practical enough to use often. You can find her on Ravelry as the Backloop.

Fair Isle

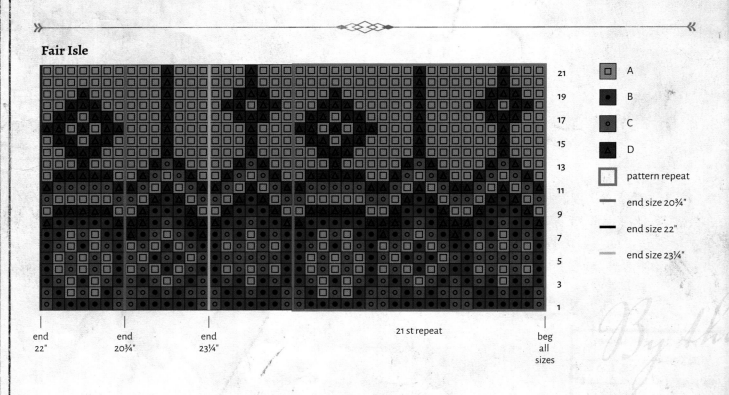

⊡	A
⚫	B
⊙	C
▲	D
☐	pattern repeat
──	end size 20¾"
━━	end size 22"
──	end size 23¼"

end 22"   end 20¾"   end 23¼"   21 st repeat   beg all sizes

Chilly Castle Socks

‡ Josie Mercier

These socks are designed especially for spending long hours in ancient, drafty castles. They are worked primarily in a specked rib pattern, whose heavy texture promises warm feet. Initials or secret messages can be worked across the top front of the sock in contrast color using duplicate stitch on a background of stockinette-stitch squares fitted neatly into the specked rib pattern.

Finished Size

7¼ (8½, 9¾)" (18.5 [21.5, 25] cm) foot circumference and 8½ (10, 11½)" (21.5 [25.5, 29] cm) foot length from back of heel to tip of toe. Socks shown measure 8½" (21.5 cm).

Yarn

Shibui Knits Staccato (65% superwash Merino, 30% silk, 5% nylon; 191 yd [175 m]/1¾ oz [50 g]): #117 artichoke (MC), 2 (2, 2) skeins; #2017 velvet (CC), 1 (1, 1) skein.

Needles

Size 2 (2.75 mm). (See Notes.) *Adjust needle size if necessary to obtain the correct gauge.*

Notions

Markers (m); tapestry needle; stitch holder (optional).

Gauge

28 sts and 40 rows = 4" (10 cm) in St st; 40 sts and 44 rows = 4" (10 cm) in Seeded Rib, relaxed.

Stitch Guide

Seeded Rib (multiple of 5 sts)

RND 1: *P1, k3, p1; rep from * to end.

RND 2: *[P1, k1] 2 times, p1; rep from * to end.

Rep Rnds 1–2.

NOTES

❋ *These socks are worked from the toe up with a short-row heel.*

❋ *The letters are worked in duplicate stitch after the socks are completed.*

❋ *Socks may be worked using a set of double-pointed needles, two circular needles, or one long circular needle as preferred.*

First Sock

Toe

Using CC, CO 28 (34, 40) sts using Judy's Magic Cast-on (see Glossary), placing 14 (17, 20) sts on each needle. Place marker (pm) and join in the rnd.

NEXT RND: K14 (17, 20), pm, knit to end.

INC RND: [K1, M1L, knit to 1 st before m, M1R, k1] 2 times—4 sts inc'd. Rep Inc Rnd on every other rnd 7 (8, 9) more times—60 (70, 80) sts. Knit 3 rnds. Change to MC.

Foot

NEXT RND: Work Seeded Rib over next 30 (35, 40) sts, knit to end. Continue in patt until piece measures 6½ (7¾, 9)" (16.5 [19.5, 23] cm) from CO, ending with Rnd 1 of Seeded Rib.

NEXT RND: Work 30 (35, 40) sts in patt and place on holder—30 (35, 40) sts rem.

Heel

Change to CC. Shape first half of heel using short-rows as foll:

SHORT-ROW 1: (RS): Knit to last st, wrap next st, turn.

SHORT-ROW 2: (WS) Purl to last st, wrap next st, turn.

SHORT-ROW 3: Knit to 1 st before previous wrapped st, wrap next st, turn.

SHORT-ROW 4: Purl to 1 st before previous wrapped st, wrap next st, turn.

Rep Short-rows 3 and 4 eight (ten, eleven) more times—10 (11, 14) unwrapped sts rem in center of heel. Shape second half of heel using short-rows as foll:

SHORT-ROW 1: (RS) Knit to first wrapped st, work wrap tog with wrapped st, wrap next st, turn.

SHORT-ROW 2: (WS) Purl to first wrapped st, work wrap tog with wrapped st, wrap next st, turn.

SHORT-ROW 3: Knit to next wrapped st, work wrap tog with wrapped st, wrap next st, turn.

SHORT-ROW 4: Purl to next wrapped st, work wrap tog with wrapped st, wrap next st, turn.

Rep Short-rows 3 and 4 seven (eight, nine) more times—28 (33, 38) unwrapped sts in center of heel. Change to MC.

NEXT RND: Working rem wraps tog with wrapped sts, work Rnd 1 of Seeded Rib to end of heel sts, place 30 (35, 40) sts from holder onto needle(s), work in established patt to end— 60 (70, 80) sts. Pm for new beg of rnd.

Leg

Continue in patt until leg measures 6½ (6¾, 7)" (16.5 [19.5, 18] cm) from point of heel, or 3½" (9 cm) less than desired length.

Letter Boxes

NEXT RND: Work 19 (24, 24) sts in patt, pm for new beg of rnd, [p2, k8] removing old m, work in patt to end.

NEXT RND: [P2, k8], work in patt to end. Rep last rnd 13 more times.

Cuff

Change to CC.

Alphabet

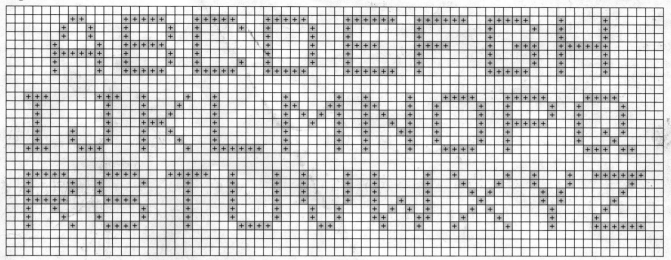

⊞ duplicate st with CC

NEXT RND: Work in k1, p1 rib, inc 8 sts evenly spaced—68 (78, 88) sts. Continue in rib until leg measures 10 (10¼, 10½)" (25.5 [26, 26.5] cm) from point of heel. BO loosely using sewn BO (see Glossary) or stretchy BO of choice.

Second Sock

Sizes 7¼ (9¾)" only
Make second sock the same as the first sock.

Size 8½" only
Work as for first sock until leg measures 6¾" (17 cm) from point of heel, or 3½" (9 cm) less than desired length.

Letter Boxes
Work 29 sts in patt, pm for new beg of rnd, [p2, k8] removing old m, work in patt to end.

NEXT RND: [P2, k8], work in patt to end. Rep last rnd 13 more times. Work cuff as for first sock.

Finishing

Weave in ends. Using CC and tapestry needle, embroider charted initials into letter boxes using duplicate stitch (see Glossary). Block to measurements. 🦉

JOSIE MERCIER has been designing knitwear since 2005, and her designs include a pair of fantasy pointed ears, a pullover with pagan influences, and a line of patterns inspired by J. R. R. Tolkien's novel *The Hobbit*. Josie lives in Belleville, Ontario, Canada, and can be found online at mercierknittingpatterns.blogspot.com or on Ravelry as Pibble.

Giant's Sweater

⚘ Anne Podlesak

This is a nice warm sweater that has some interesting details but is not overly technically difficult. Its oversize luxury makes it fit for any giant out and about on a chilly morning (though non-giants will be able to make and wear it as well!).

Finished Size

34½ (38½, 42½, 46½, 50½)" (87.5 [98, 108, 118, 128.5] cm) chest circumference. Sweater shown measures 50½" (128.5 cm).

Yarn

Knit Picks City Tweed Aran/HW (55% Merino, 25% superfine alpaca, 20% Donegal tweed; 164 yd [150 m]/3½ oz [100 g]); #24526 lemon curd, 7 (8, 9, 11, 11) skeins. Yarn distributed by Crafts Americana.

Needles

Body and sleeves—size 8 (5 mm): 32" (81.5 cm) circular (cir) and straight.

Body and sleeve ribbing—size 6 (4 mm) straight. *Neckband*—size 6 (4 mm) 12" (30.5 cm) cir or set of double-pointed (dpn). *Adjust needle size if necessary to obtain the correct gauge.*

Notions

Markers (m); cable needle (cn); tapestry needle; 3 stitch holders.

Gauge

16 sts and 24 rows = 4" (10 cm) in Dragon Scale patt, blocked; 36 st Buckbeak cable patt measures 7¼" (18.5 cm), blocked. Both are part of the Buckbeak chart.

Stitch Guide

Twisted Rib (multiple of 2 sts)

Rnd 1: *K1tbl, p1; rep from * around.

Rep Rnd 1 for patt.

Wrap 2: With right needle tip, lift strand between needles from front to back, k2, pass the lifted strand over the 2 sts just knitted.

NOTE

While incorporating the textured portion of the pattern into the sleeve increases, only work the wrap-2 stitches if there are two knit stitches to be worked after the increase. Otherwise, knit the stitches.

Back

With smaller needles, CO 67 (75, 83, 91, 99) sts.

NEXT ROW: (WS) Purl. Work Rows 1–17 of Rib chart. Change to larger needles.

NEXT ROW: (RS) [K3 (4, 5, 6, 7), k1f&b] 3 times, k5 (6, 7, 8, 9), work Set-up Row 1 of Cable chart over 33 sts, k5 (6, 7, 8, 9), [k1f&b, k3 (4, 5, 6, 7)] 3 times—76 (84, 92, 100, 108) sts.

NEXT ROW: (WS) P20 (24, 28, 32, 36), work Set-up Row 2 of cable chart over 36 sts, purl to end.

NEXT ROW: (RS) K1, work next row of cable chart to last st, k1. Working first and last st in St st, work in patt as established until piece measures 25 (26½, 27½, 28½, 29½)" (63.5 [67.5, 70, 72.5, 75] cm) from CO, ending with chart row 6, 12, 18, 24, 30, or 36.

NEXT ROW: (RS) BO 20 (24, 28, 32, 36) sts, break yarn, place the center 36 sts on a holder, join yarn and BO rem 20 (24, 28, 32, 36) sts.

Front

Work as for back until piece measures 22¼ (23¾, 24½, 25½, 26½)" (56.5 [60.5, 61.5, 65, 67.5] cm) from CO, ending with a WS row.

NEXT ROW: (RS) Work 26 (30, 34, 38, 42) sts in patt, k2tog, k1, break yarn, place center 18 sts on a holder, join new ball of yarn, k1, ssk, work in patt to end—28 (32, 36, 40, 44) sts rem each side. Place left shoulder sts on holder.

Right Front Neckline Shaping

Work 1 WS row in patt.

DEC ROW: (RS) K1, ssk, work in patt to end—1 st dec'd. Rep Dec Row every RS row 7 more times—20 (24, 28, 32,

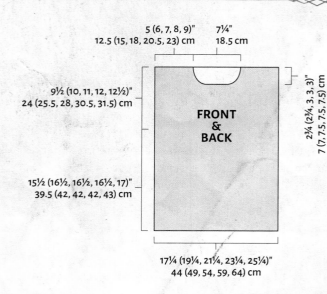

5 (6, 7, 8, 9)"
12.5 (15, 18, 20.5, 23) cm

7¼"
18.5 cm

9½ (10, 11, 12, 12½)"
24 (25.5, 28, 30.5, 31.5) cm

FRONT & BACK

2¾ (2¾, 3, 3, 3)"
7 (7, 7.5, 7.5, 7.5) cm

15½ (16½, 16½, 16½, 17)"
39.5 (42, 42, 42, 43) cm

17¼ (19¼, 21¼, 23¼, 25¼)"
44 (49, 54, 59, 64) cm

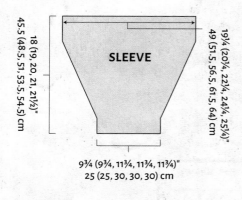

18 (19, 20, 21, 21½)"
45.5 (48.5, 51, 53.5, 54.5) cm

SLEEVE

19¼ (20¼, 22¼, 24¼, 25¼)"
49 (51.5, 56.5, 61.5, 64) cm

9¾ (9¾, 11¾, 11¾, 11¾)"
25 (25, 30, 30, 30) cm

36) sts rem. Work even in patt until right front measures 25 (26½, 27½, 28½, 29½)" (63.5 [67.5, 70, 72.5, 75] cm) from CO, ending with chart row 6, 12, 18, 24, 30, or 36. BO all rem sts.

Left Front Neckline Shaping

With WS facing, return 28 (32, 36, 40, 44) left front sts to needle and join yarn. Work 1 WS row in patt.

DEC ROW: (RS) Work in patt to last 3 sts, k2tog, k1—1 st dec'd. Rep Dec Row every RS row 7 more times—20 (24, 28, 32, 36) sts rem. Work even in patt until left front measures 25 (26½, 27½, 28½, 29½)" (63.5 [67.5, 70, 72.5, 75] cm) from CO, ending with chart row 6, 12, 18, 24, 30, or 36. BO all rem sts.

Sleeves

With smaller needles, CO 43 (43, 51, 51, 51) sts.

NEXT ROW: (WS) Purl. Work Rows 1–17 of Follow the Rib chart. Change to larger needles.

NEXT ROW: (RS) K1 (1, 2, 2, 2), [K1f&b, k0 (0, 1, 1, 1)] 3 times, k1, pm, work Set-up Row 1 of Buckbeak chart over 33 sts, pm, k1, [k0 (0, 1, 1, 1), k1f&b] 3 times, k1 (1, 2, 2, 2)—52 (52, 60, 60, 60) sts.

NEXT ROW: (WS) P8 (8, 12, 12, 12), work Set-up Row 2 of Cable chart over 36 sts, purl to end.

INC ROW: (RS) K1, M1, work next row of Cable chart to last st, M1, k1—2 sts inc'd. Rep Inc Row every 4th row 15 (17, 17, 21, 23) more times (see Notes)—84 (88, 96, 104, 108) sts. Work even in patt until sleeve measures 18 (19, 20, 21, 21½)" (45.5 [48.5, 51, 53.5, 54.5] cm) from CO, ending with chart row 6, 12, 18, 24, 30, or 36. BO all sts.

Cable

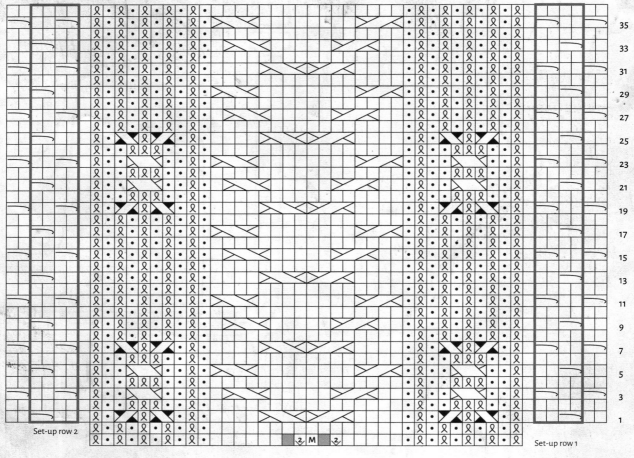

Set-up row 2

4 st repeat

35 33 31 29 27 25 23 21 19 17 15 13 11 9 7 5 3 1

Set-up row 1

4 st repeat

Rib

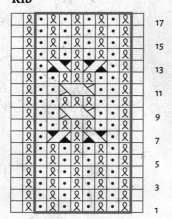

17 15 13 11 9 7 5 3 1

8 st repeat

☐	k on RS; p on WS	
•	p on RS; k on WS	
ℝ	k1tbl on RS, p1tbl on WS	
⅃	k1f&b	
M	M1	
☐	pattern repeat	
⌒	wrap 2 (see Stitch Guide)	

sl 1 st onto cn, hold in back, k1, p1 from cn

sl 1 st onto cn, hold in front, p1, k1 from cn

sl 2 sts onto cn, hold in front, k1, k2 from cn

sl 2 sts onto cn, hold in back, k2, k2 from cn

sl 2 sts onto cn, hold in front, k2, k2 from cn

Finishing

Block all pieces to measurements. Allow to dry thoroughly before unpinning. Sew shoulder seams.

Neckband

With smaller dpn or cir needle and beg at left shoulder seam, pick up and knit 7 (7, 9, 12, 12) sts along left front neck edge, k18 front neck sts from holder, pick up and knit 7 (7, 9, 12, 12) sts along right front neck edge, k36 back neck sts from holder—68 (68, 72, 78, 78) total sts. Place marker (pm) and join in the rnd. Work in Twisted Rib (see Stitch Guide) for 8 rnds. BO loosely in patt. Centering the middle of the upper edge of the sleeve at the shoulder seam, sew sleeves onto body. Sew sleeve and side seams. Weave in ends. 🐾

ANNE PODLESAK of White Rock, New Mexico, has been knitting since the squirmy age of six. She was taught to knit by her grandmother and great-aunt in an attempt to get her to sit still but didn't officially become an addict until she was in high school, at which point, there was no looking back. She is the owner of the indie dye studio, Wooly Wonka Fibers.

Enchanted Forest *Scarf*

❧ T. L. Alexandria Volk

*I*n so many fairy tales, the woods play an integral role as places of adventure, growth, and exploration. Just as a forest is a mixture of vegetation and pathway, this scarf is a deceptively simple mix of basic stitches and interwoven construction.

Finished Size

About 11" (28 cm) wide and 90" (228.5 cm) long.

Yarn

Knit Picks Chroma Worsted (70% wool, 30% nylon; 198 yd [181 m]/3½ oz [100 g]): #26164 seaweed (MC), 2 skeins. Knit Picks Wool of the Andes Tweed (80% Peruvian highland wool, 20% Donegal tweed; 110 yd [101 m]/1¾ oz [50 g]): #25448 sequoia heather tweed (CC1), 2 skeins. Knit Picks Swish Tonal (100% superwash Merino; 220 yd [201 m]/3½ oz [100 g]): #25432 canopy (CC2), 2 skeins. Knit Picks Wool of the Andes Worsted (100% wool; 110 yd [101 m]/1¾ oz [50 g]): #25647 fjord heather (CC3), 1 skein; #25989 larch heather (CC4), 2 skeins. Knit Picks Andes del Campo (100% highland wool; 164 yd [150 m]/3½ oz [100 g]): #25476 wharf heather (CC5), 1 skein. Yarn distributed by Crafts Americana.

Needles

Strip A—size 6 (4.0 mm) and size 9 (5.5 mm): straight. Strips B, C, and D—size 7 (4.5 mm): straight. Strips E, F, and G—size 8 (5.0 mm): 60" (152.5 cm) circular (cir). Strip H—size 9 (5.5 mm): straight. *Adjust needle size if necessary to obtain the correct gauge.*

Notions

Tapestry needle; cable needle (cn); yarn pins or knitter's safety pins.

Gauge

Gauge is not crucial to this project and varies with the strips and yarn used; 18 sts and 20 rows = 4" (10 cm) in St st on size 8 (5.0 mm) needles is baseline.

Stitch Guide

Ribbon Stripe

ROW 1 (AND ALL OTHER WS ROWS): Purl.

ROWS 2, 4, 6, 10, AND 12: Knit.

ROW 8: *K1f&b; rep from * to end. Change to smaller needle size as indicated.

ROW 14: *K2tog; rep from * to end. Change back to original needle size.

Rep Rows 1–14 for patt.

Cable 3 Front (C3F)

Sl 3 sts to cn, hold in front, k3, k3 from cn.

NOTE

❋ *The success of this project depends upon the mixture of color, gauge, and texture of the yarns. Each strip should vary a bit in length.*

Make the Strips

Strip A

Using MC and size 9 needles, CO 18 sts. Work in Ribbon Stripe patt until strip is about 90" (228.5 cm) long, ending on larger needles. BO all sts.

Strip B

Using MC and size 7 needles, CO 12 sts. Work in St st until strip is about 90" (228.5 cm) long. BO all sts.

Strip C

Using CC1 and size 7 needles, CO 16 sts. Work 28 rows in St st, ending with a purl row. Work cable row as foll: K5, C3F, k5.

Work 45 rows in St st.

Work cable row.

Work 23 rows in St st.

Work cable row.

Work 63 rows in St st.

Work cable row.

Work 33 rows in St st.

Work cable row.

Work 53 rows in St st.

Work cable row.

Work 29 rows in St st.

Work cable row.

Work 31 rows in St st.

Work cable row.

Work 47 rows in St st. BO all sts.

Strip D

Using CC2 and size 7 needles, CO 18 sts. Work in St st until strip is about 90" (228.5 cm) long. BO all sts.

Strip E

Using CC2 and size 8 cir, CO 400 sts. Do not join. Work in St st for 7 rows. BO all sts.

Strip F

Using CC3 and size 8 cir, CO 390 sts. Do not join. Work in St st for 7 rows. BO all sts.

Strip G

Using CC4 and size 8 cir, CO 378 sts. Do not join. Work in garter st for 20 rows. BO all sts.

Strip H

Using CC5 and size 9 needles, loosely CO 14 sts. Work in St st until strip is about 90" (228.5 cm) long. BO 3 sts, drop next st. BO 6 sts, drop next st. BO rem sts. Work dropped sts down to end of strip.

Finishing

Just as there are many ways to take a walk through the woods, there are many ways of assembling this scarf. Experimentation is the key to success! Do not block pieces. The natural roll of the fabric is important to the shape of the finished scarf. Strips E and F will curl into tubes. Lay the strips out on a table beside each other in a pleasing arrangement. Have yarn pins or knitter's safety pins at the ready. Weave and twist strips around each other, crossing 1–5 times down the length of the scarf. Let the narrowest pieces move in a serpentine manner, traveling more angularly. With pins, attach strips to each other at intervals along the length of the scarf; each stitching point should be between ½" and 2" (1.3–5 cm) long. Hold up the pinned scarf and drape it around your neck. Is the arrangement pleasing and the structure hanging together, but not stiff? If not, go back and adjust. When the arrangement is pleasing and the drape is as you like it, with appropriate yarn threaded on a tapestry needle, seam the points of contact together. Don't overseam! The scarf's movement and beauty rests in its fluid nature. Weave in ends. 🦅

T. L. ALEXANDRIA VOLK learned to knit (continental and combination) at the age of four, and the fiber arts are an integral part of her practice as a costumer, artist, milliner, writer, and teacher. She is intrigued by the tension between the construction of objects from yarn and the construction of objects from fabric and how tailoring, millinery, and older garment-fitting methods and solutions can inspire design. She is also interested in how the patterns within biology and mathematics can be a fertile ground for developing beauty and functionality for knitting and crocheting techniques. On Ravelry she is BlackSwan.

Gardener's Socks

Rachel Coopey

*I*nspired by the botanical beauty of herbs and plants, these socks are adorned with leaves and twisted vines that wind their way down.

Finished Size

6¼ (7¼, 8¼)" (16 [18.5, 21] cm) foot circumference. Will stretch to fit 8 (9, 10)" (20.5 [23, 25.5] cm), leg length 6" (15 cm). Shown in size 7¼" (18.5 cm) foot circumference.

Yarn

Malabrigo Sock (100% superwash Merino; 440 yd [402 m]/3½ oz [100 g]): #138 ivy, 1 skein.

Needles

Size 1½ (2.5 mm): set of double-pointed (dpn). *Adjust needle size if necessary to obtain the correct gauge.*

Notions

Cable needle (cn); stitch holder; tapestry needle.

Gauge

32 sts and 50 rnds = 4" (10 cm) in St st; 39 sts and 50 rnds = 4" (10 cm) in patt.

Stitch Guide

½ RC: Sl 2 sts onto cn, hold in back, k1, k2 from cn.

½ LC: Sl 1 st onto cn, hold in front, k2, k1 from cn.

Right Sock
Cuff

CO 56 (64, 72) sts. Divide sts evenly over dpn and join in the rnd.

RNDS 1–3: *[P1, k1tbl] 9 times, p2, [k3, p1] 2 (3, 4) times; rep from * once more.

RND 4: *[P1, k1tbl] 9 times, p2, [½ RC, p1] 2 (3, 4) times; rep from * once more.

Rep last 4 rnds 4 more times. Work Rnds 1–8 of Right Sock chart 8 times.

Heel flap

Heel is worked back and forth in rows over last 28 (32, 36) sts. Place rem 28 (32, 36) sts on holder for instep.

ROW 1: (WS) Sl 1 pwise with yarn in front (wyf), [p3, k1] 2 (3, 4) times, k1, p18.

ROW 2: (RS) [Sl 1 pwise with yarn in back (wyb), k1] 9 times, p2, [k3, p1] 2 (3, 4) times.

ROW 3: (WS) Sl 1 pwise wyf, [p3, k1] 2 (3, 4) times, k1, p18.

ROW 4: (RS) [Sl 1 pwise wyb, k1] 9 times, p2, [½ RC, p1] 2 (3, 4) times.

Rep last 4 rows 6 more times, then work Rows 1–3 once more.

Turn heel

Work short-rows as foll:

SHORT-ROW 1: (RS) Sl 1 pwise wyb, k16 (18, 20), ssk, k1, turn.

SHORT-ROW 2: (WS) Sl 1 pwise wyf, p7, p2tog, p1, turn.

SHORT-ROW 3: (RS) Sl 1 pwise, wyb, knit to 1 st before gap, ssk, k1, turn.

SHORT-ROW 4: (WS) Sl 1 pwise wyf, purl to 1 st before gap, p2tog, p1, turn.

Rep last 2 short-rows 3 (4, 5) more times, ending with a WS row—18 (20, 22) heel sts rem.

Gusset

Set-up rnd Sl 1 pwise wyb, k17 (19, 21), pick up and knit 16 sts along edge of heel flap (1 st in each chain-edge st), work in charted patt as established over 28 (32, 36) instep sts, pick up and knit 16 sts along edge of heel flap, k34 (36, 38)—78 (84, 90) sts. Rnd beg at instep.

DEC RND: Work in patt over 28 (32, 36) instep sts, ssk, knit to last 2 sts, k2tog—2 sts dec'd.

NEXT RND: Work in patt over instep sts, knit to end.

Rep last 2 rnds 10 (9, 8) more times—56 (64, 72) sts rem; 28 (32, 36) sts each for instep and sole.

Foot

Working in charted patt on instep sts and St st on sole sts, work even in patt until foot measures 2" (5 cm) less than desired finished length.

Toe

DEC RND: K1, ssk, knit to last 3 instep sts, k2tog, k2, ssk, knit to last 3 sole sts, k2tog, k1—4 sts dec'd.

NEXT RND: Knit.

Rep last 2 rnds 8 (10, 11) more times—20 (20, 24) sts rem. Break yarn, leaving a 12" (30.5 cm) tail.

Left Sock
Cuff

RNDS 1–3: *[P1, k3] 2 (3, 4) times, p2, [k1tbl, p1] 9 times; rep from * once more.

RND 4: *[P1, ½ LC] 2 (3, 4) times, p2, [k1tbl, p1] 9 times; rep from * once more.

Rep last 4 rnds 4 more times. Work Rnds 1–8 of Left Sock chart 8 times.

Left sock

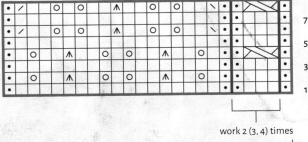

work 2 (3, 4) times

28 (32, 36) st repeat

Right sock

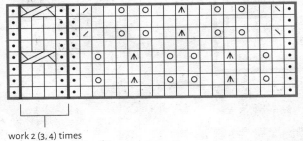

work 2 (3, 4) times

28 (32, 36) st repeat

	knit		ssk			pattern repeat
•	purl	⋀	sl 2 as if to k2tog, k1, p2sso		1/2 RC (see Stitch Guide)	
o	yo		pattern repeat		1/2 LC (see Stitch Guide)	
/	k2tog					

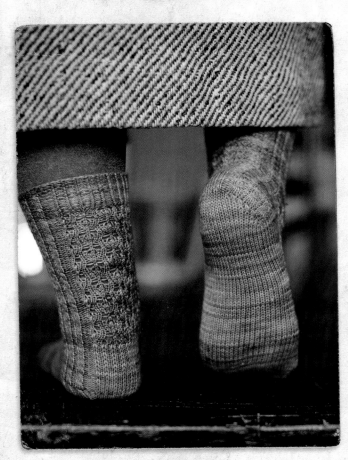

Heel Flap

Heel is worked back and forth in rows over last 28 (32, 36) sts. Place rem 28 (32, 36) sts on holder for instep.

ROW 1: (WS) Sl 1 pwise wyf, p17, k2, [p3, k1] 1 (2, 3) times, p4.

ROW 2: (RS) Sl 1 pwise wyb, [k3, p1] 2 (3, 4) times, p1, [sl 1 pwise wyb; k1] 9 times.

ROW 3: (WS) Sl 1 pwise wyf, p17, k2, [p3, k1] 1 (2, 3) times, p4.

ROW 4: (RS) Sl 1 pwise wyb, [½ LC, p1] 2 (3, 4) times, p1, [sl 1 pwise wyb; k1] 9 times.

Rep last 4 rows 6 more times, then work Rows 1–3 once more.

Turn heel and work gusset, foot, and toe as for right sock.

Finishing

With tail threaded on a tapestry needle, graft sts using Kitchener st (see Glossary). Weave in ends and block.

RACHEL COOPEY of Worcestershire, United Kingdom, loves designing and knitting socks. You can read about her constant quest for warm feet, her ever-growing sock-yarn collection, and her knitting and spinning adventures on her blog, coopknits.co.uk and find her on Ravelry as Coopknit.

Rich Earth Mitts

⚜ Jennifer Dassau

These fingerless mitts are earthy, robust, and ready for hard work cultivating magical herbs and plants. Cast on provisionally at the outer edge of the hand, they are worked flat using short-rows, then grafted for a seamless finish. The cuff is shaped into a point with increases and decreases and made to flare with a short-row wedge. The finger opening is embellished with a spiky picot edge worked by casting on and binding off stitches.

Finished Size

6½ (7½, 8¾)" (16.5 [19, 22] cm) circumference and 7½ (8½, 9½)" (19 [21.5, 24] cm) length from cuff point to tip. Mitts shown measure 6½" (16.5 cm).

Yarn

Rowan Felted Tweed DK (50% wool, 25% alpaca, 25% viscose; 191 yd [175 m]/1¾ oz [50 g]): #154 ginger, 1 ball.

Yarn distributed by Westminster Fibers.

Needles

Size 6 (4 mm). *Adjust needle size if necessary to obtain the correct gauge.*

Notions

Markers (m), 1 color A and 1 color B; scrap yarn; stitch holders; tapestry needle.

Gauge

20 sts and 40 rows = 4" (10 cm) in garter st.
Note: *Row gauge determines hand circumference, while stitch gauge determines length in this sideways knit.*

Mitt

Using provisional CO method (see Glossary), CO 29 (33, 37) sts.

SET-UP ROW: (RS) K7 (6, 5), place marker (pm) A, k19 (24, 29), pm B, k3.

NEXT ROW: CO 2 sts, BO 2 sts just cast on, knit to end.

First Side

Shape Cuff

SHORT-ROW 1: (RS) K1, k1f&b, knit to 1 st before mB, wrap next st, turn—1 st inc'd.

SHORT-ROW 2: (WS) Knit to 1 st before mA, wrap next, turn.

NEXT ROW: Knit to end.

NEXT ROW: (WS) CO 2 sts, BO 2 sts, knit to end.

INC ROW: (RS) K1, k1f&b, knit to end—1 st inc'd.

NEXT ROW: CO 2 sts, BO 2 sts, knit to end. Rep the last 6 rows 1 (2, 2) more times, then last 2 rows only 1 (0, 1) time—34 (39, 44) sts.

Work Eyelet Wedge

SHORT-ROW 1: (RS) K1, k1f&b, [yo, k2tog] 4 times, wrap next st, turn—35 (40, 45) sts.

SHORT-ROWS 2, 4, 6, 8, 10, 12, 14, 16: (WS) Knit to end.

SHORT-ROW 3: K1, k1f&b, k2, wrap next st, turn—36 (41, 46) sts.

SHORT-ROW 5: K1, k1f&b, k6, wrap next st, turn—37 (42, 47) sts.

SHORT-ROW 7: K1, k1f&b, k10, wrap next st, turn—38 (43, 48) sts.

SHORT-ROW 9: Knit to 1 st before mA, wrap next st, turn.

SHORT-ROW 11: K1, ssk, knit to 2 sts before previous wrapped st, wrap next st, turn—37 (42, 47) sts.

SHORT-ROWS 13 AND 15: K1, ssk, knit to 3 sts before previous wrapped st, wrap next st, turn—35 (40, 45) sts.

SHORT-ROW 17: K1, ssk, [yo, k2tog] 4 times, wrap next st, turn—34 (39, 44) sts.

SHORT-ROW 18: (WS) Knit to end.

Sizes 6½ (8¾)" only
NEXT ROW: (RS) K1, ssk, knit to end.

NEXT ROW: CO 2 sts, BO 2 sts, knit to end—33 (43) sts.

All Sizes
Shape Cuff

SHORT-ROW 1: (RS) K1, ssk, knit to 1 st before mB, wrap next st, turn—1 st dec'd.

SHORT-ROW 2: (WS) Knit to 1 st before mA, wrap next st, turn.

NEXT ROW: Knit to end.

NEXT ROW: CO 2 sts, BO 2 sts, knit to end.

DEC ROW: K1, ssk, knit to end—1 st dec'd.

NEXT ROW: CO 2 sts, BO 2 sts, knit to end. Rep the last 6 rows 1 (2, 2) more times—29 (33, 37) sts.

Sizes 6½ (8¾) only
Knit 1 row.

NEXT ROW: (WS) CO 2 sts, BO 2 sts, knit to end.

Thumb

NEXT ROW: (RS) Knit to last 8 (10, 12) sts, place next 8 (10, 12) sts with mB on holder; using provisional method, CO 4 sts onto right needle—25 (27, 29) sts.

Shape First Half of Thumb

SHORT-ROW 1: (WS) Knit to 1 (2, 3) sts before mA, wrap next st, turn.

SHORT-ROW 2: Knit to end.

SHORT-ROW 3: Knit to 1 st before previous wrapped st, wrap next st, turn.

NEXT ROW: (RS) Knit to last 4 sts, place next 4 sts on a separate holder, transfer 8 (10, 12) sts from first holder to needle and knit across—29 (33, 37) sts.

NEXT ROW: CO 2 sts, BO 2 sts, knit to end.

Second Side

Work as for First Side. Cut yarn, leaving a 20" (51 cm) tail for grafting.

Finishing

Graft CO hand sts to live sts on needle as foll: Place 29 (33, 37) sts from provisional CO on second needle, removing waste yarn as you go. Holding needle with CO sts in back (BN) and needle with live sts in front (FN), thread tail onto tapestry needle. Graft in garter st:

Step 1: Insert tapestry needle pwise into first st on FN, draw yarn through, leave st on FN.

Step 2: Insert tapestry needle kwise into first st on BN, remove st onto tapestry needle, but do not draw yarn through until next step.

Step 3: Insert tapestry needle pwise into next st on BN, draw yarn through, leave st on BN.

Step 4: Insert tapestry needle kwise into first st on FN, remove st onto tapestry needle, but do not draw yarn through until next step.

Rep Steps 1–4.

Graft CO thumb sts to held sts as foll: Place 4 sts from provisional CO onto needle, removing waste yarn as you go. Place 4 held sts onto second needle. Holding needle with CO sts in back (BN) and needle with held sts in front (FN), using a new length of yarn threaded on tapestry needle, rep Steps 1–4 as for hand. Weave in ends.

Blocking is not necessary, as the textural garter stitch and uneven quality of the yarn enhances Pomona's particular charm. 🦉

JENNIFER DASSAU is a recovering attorney and emigrée from Seventh Avenue (Manhattan), who never misses an opportunity to design with short-rows. Find her in The Knitting Vortex atjenniferdassau.com and on Ravelry as knittingvortex.

SHORT-ROW 4: Knit to end.

Rep Short-rows 3 and 4 two (three, four) more times. Knit 2 rows.

Shape Second Half of Thumb

SHORT-ROW 1: (WS) Knit to 4 (6, 8) sts before mA, wrap next st, turn.

SHORT-ROW 2: Knit to end.

SHORT-ROW 3: Knit to previous wrapped st, knit wrapped st, wrap next st, turn.

SHORT-ROW 4: Knit to end.

Rep Short-rows 3 and 4 two (three, four) more times. Knit 1 row.

Shimmering *Cloak*

⟡ Joanna Johnson

This design pays homage to any unassuming piece of fabric with great magical powers. The blend of alpaca and silk yarn creates a wonderfully fluid drape, and its name, Metalico, aptly describes its seemingly metallurgical shimmer, which is a key component of this design. The unisex cloak mimics chain mail and is suitable for an advanced beginning knitter.

Finished Size

37¾ (41½, 45¾)" (96 [105.5, 116] cm) to fit size 32 (36, 40)" (81.5 [91.5, 101.5] cm) chest circumference, 20 (22½, 25½)" (51 [57, 65] cm) neck circumference, 46½ (50¼, 54½)" (118 [127.5, 138] cm) lower edge circumference, and 28" (71 cm) tall. Cloak shown measures 37¾" (96 cm).

Yarn

Blue Sky Alpacas Metalico (50% baby alpaca, 50% raw silk; 147 yd [135 m]/1¾ oz [50 g]): #1612 platinum, 8 (9, 11) skeins.

Needles

Size 5 (3.75 mm): 24" circular (cir). *Adjust needle size if necessary to obtain the correct gauge.*

Notions

Markers (m); one ½" button.

Gauge

22 sts and 29 rows = 4" (10 cm) in St st; 22 sts and 29 rows = 4" (10 cm) in pattern st.

Stitch Guide

S2KP2: Sl 2 sts as if to k2tog, k1, pass 2 slipped sts over the knit st—2 sts dec'd.

Star Rib Mesh (worked over 25 sts)

ROW 1: (RS) K1, [yo, s2kp2, yo, k1] 6 times.

ROW 2: Purl.

ROW 3: Ssk, yo, k1, [yo, s2kp2, yo, k1] 5 times, yo, k2tog.

ROW 4: Purl.

Rep Rows 1–4 for patt.

NOTES

✳ *This cloak is worked seamlessly in one piece from the hem up and is secured with a single button at the neck. If you wish to make the cloak longer, you may do so as indicated in the instructions.*

✳ *Slip the first stitch of every row purlwise with yarn in front.*

Cloak

CO 192 (207, 225) sts.

NEXT ROW: (WS) Sl 1, knit to end. Rep last row 5 more times, ending with a RS row.

INC ROW: (WS) Sl 1, [k1f&b, k2] 63 (68, 74) times, k1f&b, k1—256 (276, 300) sts. Set-up row (RS) Sl 1, k4, place marker (pm), k17 (21, 26), pm, k25, pm, k39 (43, 48), pm, k25, pm, k34 (38, 42), pm, k25, pm, k39 (43, 48), pm, k25, pm, k17 (21, 26), pm, k5.

NEXT ROW: (WS) Sl 1, k4, purl to last 5 sts, k5.

NEXT ROW: (RS) Sl 1, k4, sl m, [sl 1 pwise with yarn in back (wyb), knit to 1 st before next m, sl 1 pwise wyb, sl m, work in Star Rib Mesh (see Stitch Guide) over next 25 sts, sl m] 4 times, sl 1 pwise wyb, knit to 1 st before next m, sl 1 pwise wyb, sl m, k5.

NEXT ROW: (WS) Sl 1, k4, purl to last 5 sts, k5. Work in patt as established for 24 rows.

DEC ROW: (RS) Sl 1, k4, sl m, sl 1 pwise wyb, [knit to 3 sts before next m, k2tog, sl 1 pwise wyb, sl m, work in Star Rib Mesh over next 25 sts, sl m, sl 1 pwise wyb, ssk] 4 times, knit to 1 st before next m, sl 1 pwise wyb, sl m, k5—8 sts dec'd. Rep Dec Row every 24th row 5 more times—208 (228, 252) sts rem. Work even in patt for 23 rows, ending with a WS row.

Note: *Lengthen by working more rows even here if desired.*

Work Dec Row. Work 3 rows even. Rep last 4 rows 5 more times, removing m(s) on the final (WS) row—160 (180, 204) sts rem.

Hood

INC ROW: (RS) Sl 1, k4, pm, k10 (17, 25), pm, k25, pm, (k2, k1f&b) 10 times, pm, k25, pm, k10 (17, 25), pm, k5—120 (134, 150) sts.

NEXT ROW: (WS) Sl 1, k4, purl to last 5 sts, k5.

NEXT ROW: (RS) Sl 1, k4, [sl 1 pwise wyb, knit to 1 st before next m, sl 1 pwise wyb, sl m, work in Star Rib Mesh over 25 sts, sl m] 2 times, sl 1 pwise wyb, knit to 1 st before next m, sl 1 pwise wyb, sl m, k5.

NEXT ROW: (WS) Sl 1, k4, purl to last 5 sts, k5. Work in patt as established until hood measures 10¾" (27.5 cm), ending with Row 1 of Star Rib Mesh patt.

NEXT ROW: (WS) Sl 1, k4, p55 (62, 70), pm, purl to last 5 sts, k5.

Shape Hood

DEC ROW: (RS) Sl 1, k4, sl m, sl 1 pwise wyb, knit to 1 st before next m, sl 1 pwise wyb, sl m, work in Star Rib Mesh over 25 sts, sl m, sl 1 pwise wyb, knit to 3 sts before next m, k2tog, k1, sl m, k1, ssk, work in patt to end—2 sts dec'd. Rep Dec Row every 4th row 4 more times—110 (124, 140) sts rem. Rep Dec Row every RS row 10 times, ending with a RS row—90 (104, 120) sts rem. Divide hood sts in half, and graft the top of the hood tog using Kitchener stitch (see Glossary).

Finishing

Weave in ends. Block to measurements. Sew button on opposite buttonhole. ❋

JOANNA JOHNSON is the author and pattern designer of *Green Gables Knits* (Slate Falls Press, 2013) as well as of knitting storybooks *Phoebe's Sweater*, *Freddie's Blanket*, and *Phoebe's Birthday* (Slate Falls Press, 2010, 2011, 2012). She lives in a little house with big shelves full of books, fabric, and yarn in Loveland, Colorado, with her husband and their three children. She and her illustrator husband own Slate Falls Press (slatefallspress.com) and are always dreaming up more book ideas.

Shape Neckline

DEC ROW: (RS) Sl 1, k4, *k1, k2tog; rep from * to last 5 (7, 7) sts, k5 (7, 7)—110 (124, 140) sts rem.

NEXT ROW: (WS) Sl 1, knit to end. Rep last row 4 more times.

BUTTONHOLE ROW: (RS) Sl 1, k3, yo, k2tog, knit to end.

NEXT ROW: (WS) Sl 1, knit to end. Rep last row 2 more times, ending with a WS row.

Ghostly Cloak

⁜ Bethany Hick

*A*nyone with even a casual history of conjuring the dead knows that when spirits finally do appear, they prefer to wear cloaks. This cloak is intended as a modern update to the cloaks worn by millenia of spirits, made diaphanous to give a ghostly halo to the Earth-bound wearer.

Finished Size

49½ (56¼, 63)" (125.5 [143, 160] cm) circumference at lower edge, 20¾" (52.5 cm) neck circumference, and 17½ (18½, 20¼)" (44.5 [47, 51.5] cm) tall. Cloak shown measures 49½" (125.5 cm) lower edge circumference.

Yarn

Classic Elite Yarns Giselle (64% kid mohair, 25% wool, 11% nylon; 230 yd [210 m]/1¾ oz [50 g]): #4193 porcelain blue, 3 (3, 4) skeins.

Needles

Size 5 (3.75 mm): 24" (61 cm) circular (cir). *Adjust needle size if necessary to obtain the correct gauge.*

Notions

Markers (m); 2½ yd (2.3 m) 1" (2.5 cm) navy satin ribbon; 2½ yd (2.3 m) ¼" (6 mm) silver ribbon; tapestry needle; school glue.

Gauge

13½ sts and 26 rows = 4" (10 cm) in St st; 22-st lace rep measures 6¾" (17 cm).

Cloak

Using the long-tail method (see Glossary), CO 161 (183, 205) sts. Do not join.

ROW 1: (RS) Sl 1 pwise with yarn in back (wyb), *p1, k1; rep from * to end.

ROW 2: (WS) Sl 1 pwise with yarn in front (wyf), *p1, k1; rep from * to end. Rep last 2 rows once more. Work Rows 1–61 of the Lace Motif chart.

NEXT ROW: (WS) Sl 1 pwise wyf, p1, k1, purl to last 4 sts, [p1, k1] twice.

NEXT ROW: (RS) Sl 1 pwise wyb, p1, k1, p1, knit to last 4 sts, [p1, k1] twice. Work 7 (9, 13) more rows in patt as established, ending with a WS row.

DEC ROW: (RS) Sl 1 pwise wyb, p1, k1, p1, k3 (0, 2), *k2tog, k3; rep from * to last 4 sts, [p1, k1] twice—131 (148, 166) sts rem. Work 9 (11, 15) rows even in patt, ending with a WS row.

DEC ROW: (RS) Sl 1 pwise wyb, p1, k1, p1, k3 (0, 2), *k2tog, k2; rep from * to last 4 sts, [p1, k1] twice—101 (113, 127) sts rem. Work 9 (11, 15) rows even in patt, ending with a WS row.

DEC ROW: (RS) Sl 1 pwise wyb, p1, k1, p1, k0 (0, 2), *k2tog, k1; rep from * to last 4 sts, [p1, k1] twice—70 (78, 88) sts rem. Work 7 rows even in patt, ending with a WS row.

NEXT ROW: (RS) Sl 1 pwise wyb, p1, k1, p1, dec 0 (8, 18) sts evenly, knit to last 4 sts, [p1, k1] twice—70 sts rem. Work 4 rows even in patt, ending with a RS row. Beg with a WS row, work Rows 1–3 of Neck Eyelet chart. Working edge sts in patt as established, work 4 rows in St st, ending with a WS row.

Hood

INC ROW: (RS) Sl 1 pwise wyb, p1, k1, p1, k2, *M1, k2; rep from * to last 4 sts, [p1, k1] twice—100 sts. Working edge sts in patt as established, work 17 rows even in St st, ending with a WS row.

INC ROW: (RS) Sl 1 pwise wyb, p1, k1, p1, k2, *M1, k3; rep from * to last 4 sts, [p1, k1] twice—130 sts. Work 17 rows even in patt, ending with a WS row. Set-up row (RS) Sl 1 pwise wyb, p1, k1, p1, k30, place marker (pm), k2tog, k58, ssk, pm, k30, [p1, k1] twice—128 sts rem. Work 1 WS row even in patt.

DEC ROW: (RS) Sl 1 pwise wyb, p1, k1, p1, k30, sl m, k2tog, knit to 2 sts before m, ssk, sl m, k30, [p1, k1] twice—2 sts dec'd. Rep Dec Row every RS row 28 more times—70 sts rem. Cut yarn, leaving a 36" (91.5 cm) tail for grafting.

Finishing

With tail threaded on a tapestry needle, graft top of hood using Kitchener st (see Glossary). Weave in ends and block to measurements. Once dry, weave ribbons through the eyelets at the neck. To finish the ribbons, apply a small amount of school glue to the cut edge to keep the ribbons from raveling. 🦁

BETHANY HICK, who lives in northern Virginia, is a software developer for a local school system. She has always been a lover of mythology and fairy tales and always has an e-reader in her purse. When not knitting, she can be found on many local soccer fields captaining her team.

Neck Eyelet

4 st repeat

	k on RS; p on WS		/	k2tog
•	p on RS; k on WS		\	ssk
V	sl 1 wyb on RS; sl 1 wyf on WS		▢	pattern repeat
O	yo			

Lace Motif

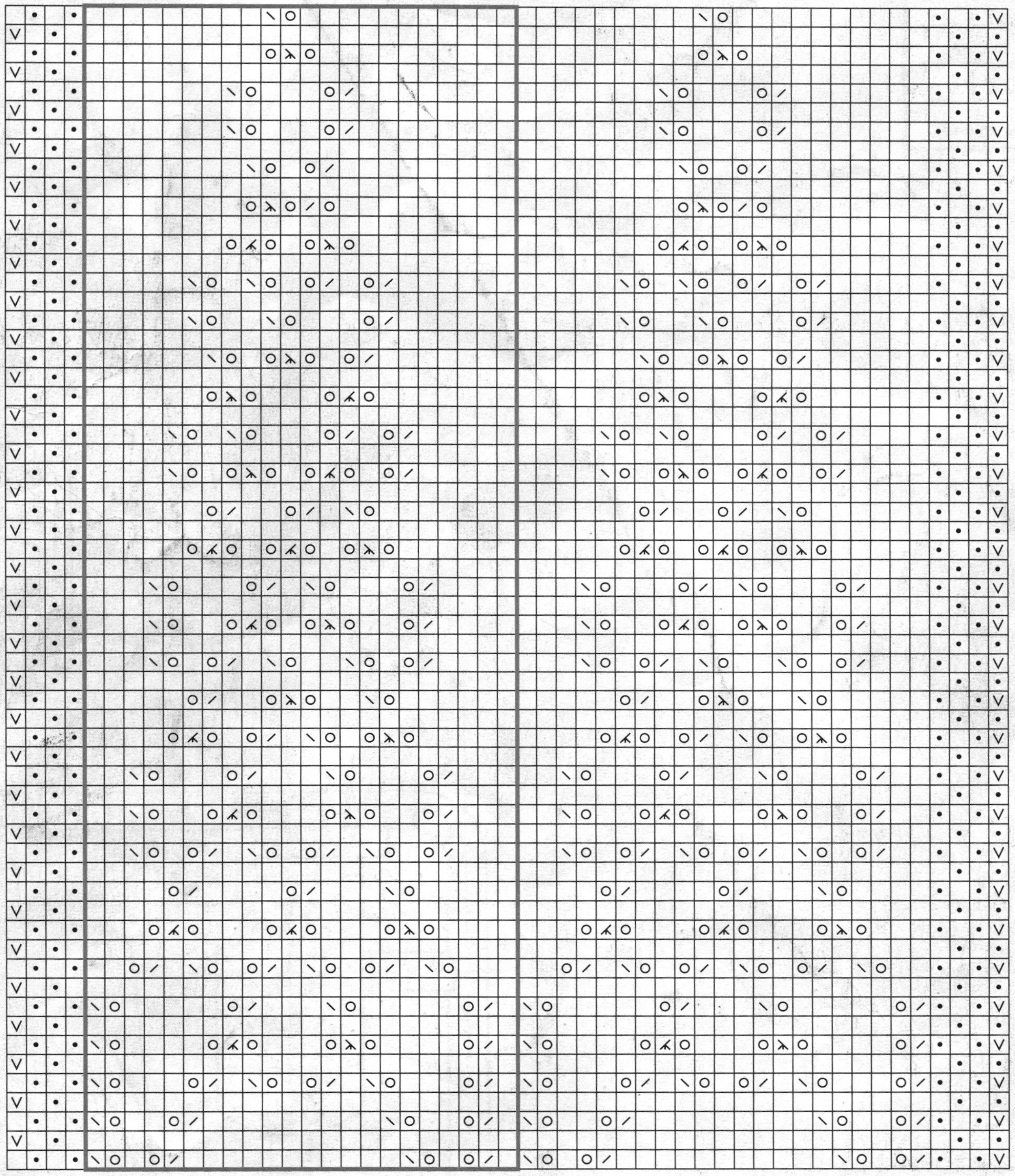

61
59
57
55
53
51
49
47
45
43
41
39
37
35
33
31
29
27
25
23
21
19
17
15
13
11
9
7
5
3
1
22 st repeat

- k on RS; p on WS
- • p on RS; k on WS
- V sl 1 wyb on RS; sl 1 wyf on WS
- O yo
- / k2tog
- \ ssk
- k3tog
- sssk (see Glossary)
- pattern repeat

Spell-Casting Mitts

✥ Anne Podlesak

Wizards in colder climates need to wear mittens or gloves to prevent wand slippage. The solution: these fun-to-knit mitts. They have fully fashioned decreases to shape the mitts over the back of the hands and sparkling corset-style lace-up ties. While size is not critical for these mitts, choose a size that most closely matches your arm circumference around the forearm. The length may be customized as you knit by adding or subtracting rows before the hand decreases.

Finished Size

8 (9, 10)" (20.5 [23, 25.5] cm) circumference; 9½ (9¾, 10)" (24 [25, 25.5] cm) in length from cuff to tip of back-of-hand shaping. Sample mitts shown in size 8" (20.5 cm).

Yarn

Debbie Bliss Rialto DK (100% Merino superwash; 115 yd [105 m]/1¾ oz [50 g]); #23044 gray (MC), 1 (2, 2) skein(s). Debbie Bliss Party Angel (72% mohair, 24% silk, 4% metallic polyester; 220 yd [201 m]/⅞ oz [25 g]): #15503 gray (CC), 1 skein.

Yarn distributed by Knitting Fever.

Needles

Body—size 6 (4 mm): 16" (40.5 cm) circular (cir); *I-cord edging and ties*—size 4 (3.5 mm): double-pointed (dpn). *Adjust needle size if necessary to obtain the correct gauge.*

Notions

Removable/coil-less safety pin markers (m), tapestry needle.

Gauge

19 sts and 28 rows = 4" (10 cm) in k2, p2 rib on larger needles, slightly stretched.

Mitt

With CC and dpn, CO 4 sts. Work I-cord (see Glossary) for 50 (56, 62)" (127 [142, 157.5] cm). BO all sts. Fold I-cord in half to find the midpoint and place removable marker. Place removable marker 4 (4½, 5)" (10 [11.5, 12.5] cm) from each side of midpoint. Remove midpoint m. With back side of the I-cord facing, using MC, cir needle, and beg at the first m, pick up and knit 38 (42, 46) sts evenly to next m. Do not join.

NEXT ROW: (WS) *P2, k2; rep from * to last 2 sts, p2. Work 10 rows in rib patt as established.

EYELET ROW: (RS) K2, BO 2 sts, work in rib patt as established to last 4 sts, BO 2 sts, k2.

NEXT ROW: (WS) P2, using the backward-loop method (see Glossary) to CO 2 sts, work in rib patt as established to last 2 sts, CO 2 sts, p2. Rep last 12 rows 3 more times—4 eyelets on each side of the mitt. Work 6 rows even in patt, ending with a WS row.

Hand Decreases

DEC ROW: (RS) K1, sssk, work in rib until the last 4 sts, k3tog, k1—4 sts dec'd.

Work 1 WS row in patt. Rep last 2 rows 7 (8, 9) more times—6 sts rem.

NEXT ROW: K1, ssk, k3tog—3 sts rem. Using these 3 sts, work I-cord for 4" (10 cm) or desired length of finger loop. BO all sts. Break yarn, leaving a 12" (30.5 cm) tail.

Finishing

With tail threaded on tapestry needle, sew the loose end of the finger loop securely to WS of mitts. Weave in ends. To block, allow mitts to soak in a lukewarm bath and then press or gently spin out excess water. Lay flat, patting the rib into place gently. Do not stretch the rib out, or it will lose its elasticity. Once fully dry, thread the ends of the lacings through the eyelet holes along the sides of the mitts. Adjust laces to fit as desired and then secure ends in a simple tie on the underside of the wrist. 🦅

ANNE PODLESAK of White Rock, New Mexico, has been knitting since the squirmy age of six. She was taught to knit by her grandmother and great-aunt in an attempt to get her to sit still but didn't officially become an addict until she was in high school, at which point, there was no looking back. She is the owner of the indie dye studio, Wooly Wonka Fibers.

A Cap Full of Caps

⚜ Kendra Nitta

Too distracted by your myriad magic-related duties to settle on one style of cap to wear? No problem! This riot of textures and colors looks like five separate hats, but through the magic of knitting is really one continuous piece. Short-rows tilt each section at an angle to make the hat look even more jumbled together. This cap is perfect for leftover yarn scraps, with each hat section using less than an ounce.

Finished Size

15½ (17, 18½)" (39.5 [43, 47] cm) brim circumference and 10¾ (11½, 12)" (27.5 [29, 30.5] cm) long. Hat shown measures 17" (43 cm). Hat is intended to be asymmetrical, so length is approximate.

Yarn

Spud & Chloë Fine (80% superwash wool, 20% silk; 248 yd [227 m]/2¼ oz [65 g]): #7818 green bean (A), #7819 orangutan (B), a7811 bumble bee (C), #7805 anemone (D), #7804 cricket (E), #7820 wildberries (F), #7800 popcorn (G), #7817 goldfish (H), 1 skein each.

Yarn distributed by Blue Sky Alpacas.

Needles

Size 3 (3.25 mm): 16" (40.5 cm) circular (cir) and set of double-pointed (dpn); size 4 (3.5 mm): 16" (40.5 cm) cir. *Adjust needle size if necessary to obtain the correct gauge.*

Notions

Markers (m); cable needle (cn); tapestry needle.

Gauge

28 sts and 36 rows = 4" (10 cm) in St st on smaller cir needle. 31 sts and 40 rows = 4" (10 cm) in k2, p2 rib on smaller cir needle, relaxed.

Stitch Guide

C6B: Sl 3 sts onto cn and hold in back, k3, k3 from cn.

NOTES

✳ *Hats 1, 3, and 4 begin with the long-tail cast-on for ribbing, demonstrated by Eunny Jang in this Knitting Daily video: knittingdaily.com/blogs/ daily/archive/2010/10/6/cast-on-with-eunny .aspx. This cast-on produces a lovely edge that creates an unbroken line of knits and purls on each side. You can also use any stretchy cast-on, such as the Old Norwegian (also known as Twisted German) cast-on.*

✳ *When working the final round of Hats 1–4, don't worry if you end up with small holes. These holes will be covered up by the bottom edge of the hat that is joined above it.*

Hat 1

With A and smaller cir needle, using the long-tail CO for ribbing and working in k2, p2 pattern (see Notes), CO 120 (132, 144) sts. Place marker (pm) and join in the rnd. Work k2, p2 rib until hat measures 1 (1¼, 1¼)" (2.5 [3.2, 3.2] cm) from CO.

Short-Row Shaping

SHORT-ROW 1: (RS) Work in patt to last 10 (15, 15) sts, wrap next st, turn.

SHORT-ROW 2: (WS) Work in patt to last 10 (15, 15) sts, wrap next st, turn.

SHORT-ROWS 3–6: Work in patt to 6 (6, 7) sts before previous wrapped st, wrap next st, turn.

SHORT-ROW 7: Knit to 6 (6, 7) sts before previous wrapped st, wrap next st, turn.

SHORT-ROW 8: Purl to 6 (6, 7) sts before previous wrapped st, wrap next st, turn.

SHORT-ROWS 9–10: Rep Short-rows 7 and 8.

NEXT RND: Work sts as they appear (knit the knit sts and purl the purl sts) to end of rnd, working wraps tog with wrapped sts.

NEXT RND: Knit, working rem wraps tog with wrapped sts. Remove m. Sl 52 (58, 63) sts pwise, leave sts on needle. Break yarn.

Hat 2

With B and larger cir needle, CO 132 (144, 156) sts. Pm and join in the rnd. Work in St st for 1" (2.5 cm). Place hat 1 inside hat 2 so that the left needle for hat 1 is directly behind the left needle for hat 2.

NEXT RND: *[Knit first st of hat 2 tog with first st of hat 1] 10 (11, 12) times, k1 from hat 2 needle only; rep from * to end—132 (144, 156) sts.

Change to smaller cir needle and knit 1 rnd.

Short-Row Shaping

SHORT-ROW 1: (RS) Knit to last 10 (15, 15) sts, wrap next st, turn.

SHORT-ROW 2: (WS) Purl to last 10 (15, 15) sts, wrap next st, turn. Break yarn B. Join C.

SHORT-ROW 3: Knit to 6 (6, 7) sts before previous wrapped st, wrap next st, turn.

SHORT-ROW 4: Purl to 6 (6, 7) sts before previous wrapped st, wrap next st, turn.

SHORT-ROWS 5–6: Rep Short-rows 3 and 4. Break yarn C. Join B.

SHORT-ROWS 7–8: Rep Short-rows 3 and 4. Break yarn B. Join C.

SHORT-ROWS 9–12: Rep Short-rows 3 and 4 twice. Break yarn C. Join B.

SHORT-ROWS 13–14: Rep Short-rows 3 and 4.

NEXT RND: Knit to end, working wraps tog with wrapped sts.

NEXT RND: Knit, working rem wraps tog with wrapped sts. Remove m. Sl 85 (95, 101) sts pwise, leave sts on needle. Break yarn. This is now the hat body.

Wave

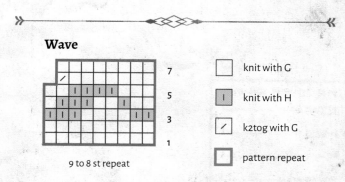

9 to 8 st repeat

- ☐ knit with G
- ▨ knit with H
- ⧄ k2tog with G
- ☐ pattern repeat

Hat 3

With D and larger cir needle, using the long-tail CO for ribbing (see Notes) and working in k6, p1 pattern, CO 154 (168, 182) sts. Pm and join in the rnd. Work in k6, p1 rib for 3 rnds.

CABLE RND: *K6, p1, C6B (see Stitch Guide), p1; rep from * to end. Place hat body inside hat 3 so that the left needle for hat body is directly behind left needle for hat 3. *[Knit first st of hat 3 tog with first st of hat body] 6 times, p1 from hat 3 needle only; rep from * to end.

Short-Row Shaping

SHORT-ROW 1: (RS) [K6, p1] 20 (22, 24) times, wrap next st, turn.

SHORT-ROW 2: (WS) [K1, p6] 18 (20, 22) times, wrap next st, turn.

SHORT-ROW 3: [C6B, p1, k6, p1] 8 (9, 10) times, C6B, p1, wrap next st, turn.

SHORT-ROWS 4, 6, 8, 10, 12, AND 14: (WS) *K1, p6; rep from * to 7 sts before previous wrapped st, wrap next st, turn.

SHORT-ROW 5: [C6B, p1, k6, p1] 7 (8, 9) times, C6B, p1, wrap next st, turn.

SHORT-ROW 7: [K6, p1] 12 (14, 16) times, wrap next st, turn.

SHORT-ROW 9: [K6, p1, C6B, p1] 5 (6, 7) times, k6, p1, wrap next st, turn.

SHORT-ROW 11: [K6, p1, C6B, p1] 4 (5, 6) times, k6, p1, wrap next st, turn.

SHORT-ROW 13: [K6, p1] 6 (8, 10) times, wrap next st, turn.

Sizes 17 (18½)" only

SHORT-ROW 15: [C6B, p1, k6, p1] 3 (4) times, k6, p1, wrap next st, turn.

SHORT-ROW 16: [K1, p6] 5 (6) times.

All Sizes

NEXT RND: [C6B, p1, k6, p1] 3 (3, 4) times, *k6, p1; rep from * to end. Change to smaller cir needle.

DEC RND: *K5, ssk; rep from * to end—132 (144, 156) sts rem. Remove m. Sl 68 (75, 81) pwise, leave sts on needle. Break yarn.

Hat 4

With E and larger cir needle, using the long-tail CO for ribbing and working in k3, p3 pattern, CO 132 (144, 156) sts. Pm and join in the rnd. Work k3, p3 rib until hat measures 1" (2.5 cm) from CO. Knit 1 rnd. Work 3 rnds k3, p3 rib. Place hat body inside hat 4 so that the left needle for hat body is directly behind the left needle for hat 4. *Knit first st of hat 4 tog with first st of hat body; rep from * to end. Change to smaller cir needle and work 3 rnds k3, p3 rib.

SHORT-ROW 1: (RS) Work in patt to last 15 sts, wrap next st, turn.

SHORT-ROW 2: Work in patt to last 15 sts, wrap next st, turn.

SHORT-ROWS 3–6: Work in patt to 9 sts before previous wrapped st, wrap next st, turn.

NEXT RND: Work in patt to end, working wraps tog with wrapped sts.

DEC RND: *Work 10 sts in patt, p2tog; rep from * to end—121 (132, 143) sts rem. Work 1 rnd even.

DEC RND: *Work 9 (10, 11) sts in patt, k2tog; rep from * to end—110 (121, 132) sts rem. Transfer sts to larger cir needle to hold. Break yarn.

Hat 5

With F and smaller cir needle, CO 110 (121, 132) sts. Purl 2 rnds. Place hat body inside hat 5 so that the left needle for hat body is directly behind the left needle for hat 5. *Knit first st of hat 5 tog with first st of hat body; rep from * to end. Knit 1 rnd.

SET-UP RND: *K11, pm; rep from * to end.

DEC RND: *Knit to 2 sts before m, k2tog; rep from * to end—100 (110, 120) sts rem. Work 5 rnds even. Rep Dec Rnd—90 (99, 108) sts rem. Break F. Using G and H, work Rnds 1–7 of Wave chart—80 (88, 96) sts rem. Change to F and work 4 (4, 9) rnds even. Rep Dec Rnd—70 (77, 84) sts rem. Rep Dec Rnd every 6th rnd 6 more times—10 (11, 12) sts rem. Break yarn, draw tail through rem sts. Pull tight to gather sts and fasten off on WS.

Finishing

With H, make a 2" (5 cm) pom-pom (see Glossary). Secure pom-pom to top of hat. Weave in ends. Steam-block, taking care to slightly unroll the edges of hats 2 and 3, and set the fold of hat 4. 🍂

KENDRA NITTA has been featured in numerous books and magazines, including Jane Austen Knits and Interweave Knits Holiday Gifts 2010. Follow her knitting, sewing, and designing adventures at missknitta.com.

Inverse Socks

✷ Rachel Coopey

When you are working on casting spells it is important to remember that, while you are working toward a desired outcome, if you aren't careful, the opposite outcome could just as easily come to pass. The lesson of these socks is that opposites are deeply linked and have an ongoing relationship over time.

Finished Size

7½ (8½, 9½)" (19 [21.5, 24] cm) foot circumference; foot length is adjustable. Will stretch to fit foot circumference 8½ (9½, 10½)" (21.5 [24, 26.5] cm), leg length 6½" (16.5 cm). Shown in size 8½" (21.5 cm) foot circumference.

Yarn

Three Irish Girls Adorn Sock (80% Merino, 20% nylon; 430 yd [393 m]/3½ oz [100 g]): Padraig and Lucky Penny, 1 skein each.

Needles

Size 1½ (2.5 mm): set of double-pointed (dpn). *Adjust needle size if necessary to obtain the correct gauge.*

Notions

Stitch holder; tapestry needle.

Gauge

30 sts and 44 rnds = 4" (10 cm) in St st; 36 sts and 44 rnds = 4" (10 cm) in rib patt.

Sock

Cuff

With color 1, CO 64 (72, 80) sts. Divide sts evenly over dpn and join in the rnd.

NEXT RND: *K1tbl, p1; rep from * to end. Cont in rib patt as established for 15 more rnds.

Leg

Work Rnds 1–6 of Cuff chart 4 times, then work Rnd 1 once more. Use color 2 for the rem sock. Work Rnds 1–4 of Rib chart 7 times, then work Rnds 1–3 once more.

Heel Flap

Set-up rnd Work Rnd 4 of Rib chart to last 0 (2, 4) sts.

Heel is worked back and forth in rows over last 33 (37, 41) sts. Place rem 31 (35, 39) sts on holder for instep.

ROW 1: (WS) Sl 1 pwise with yarn in front (wyf), p32 (36, 40).

ROW 2: (RS) *Sl 1 pwise with yarn in back (wyb), k1; rep from * to last st, k1.

Rep last 2 rows 15 more times.

Turn Heel

Work short-rows as foll:

ROW 1: (RS) Sl 1 pwise wyb, k17 (19, 21), ssk, k1, turn.

ROW 2: (WS) Sl 1 pwise wyf, p4, p2tog, p1, turn.

ROW 3: (RS) Sl 1 pwise wyb, knit to 1 st before gap, ssk, k1, turn.

ROW 4: (WS) Sl 1 pwise wyf, purl to 1 st before gap, p2tog, p1, turn.

Rep last 2 rows 5 (6, 7) more times, ending with a WS row—19 (21, 23) heel sts rem.

Gusset

SET-UP RND: Sl 1 pwise wyb, k18 (20, 22), pick up and knit 16 sts along edge of heel flap (1 st in each chain-edge st); beg and ending where indicated for your size, work Instep chart over 31 (35, 39) instep sts, pick up and knit 16 sts along edge of heel flap, k35 (37, 39)—82 (88, 94) sts. Rnd beg at instep.

DEC RND: Work in patt over 31 (35, 39) instep sts, ssk, knit to last 2 sts, k2tog—2 sts dec'd.

NEXT RND: Work in patt over instep sts, knit to end.

Rep last 2 rnds 9 (8, 7) more times—62 (70, 78) sts rem; 31 (35, 39) sts each for instep and sole.

Cuff

5
3
1

8 st repeat

Rib

3
1

8 st repeat

Instep

3
1

end
8½"

8 st repeat
work 3 times

beg
8½"

end
9½"

end
7½"

beg
7½"

beg
9½"

⊠ color 1	☐ pattern repeat
☐ color 2	▬ size 7½"
• purl	▬ size 8½"
ℓ k1tbl	▬ size 9½"

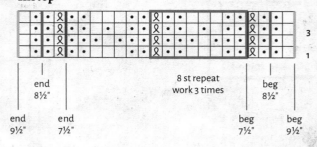

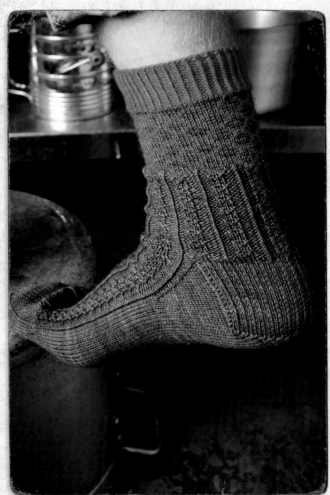

Foot

Working in charted patt on instep sts and St st on sole sts, work even in patt until foot measures 2" (5 cm) less than desired finished length.

Toe

DEC RND: K1, ssk, knit to last 3 sts of instep, k2tog, k2, ssk, knit to last 3 sts of sole, k2tog, k1—4 sts dec'd.

NEXT RND: Knit.

Rep last 2 rnds 10 (11, 13) more times—18 (22, 22) sts rem. Break yarn, leaving a 12" (30.5 cm) tail.

Finishing

With tail threaded on a tapestry needle, use Kitchener st (see Glossary) to graft sts tog. Weave in ends and block.

RACHEL COOPEY of Worcestershire, United Kingdom, loves designing and knitting socks. You can read about her constant quest for warm feet, her ever-growing sock-yarn collection, and her knitting and spinning adventures on her blog, coopknits.co.uk and find her on Ravelry as Coopknit.

Mermaid's Song

❧ Susanna IC

This shawl is inspired by the world of mermaids, those magical and dangerous dwellers of the deep. First, the deep border is knitted in one piece, side to side. The border mimics the movement and texture of waves by combining cables with lace. The open lace along the bottom edge imitates the sinuous movement of underwater plants, and the elongated beads glimmer and shine in sunlight much like water droplets. After the border is completed, stitches are picked up along the top edge, and the shawl is shaped into a crescent with a set of simple stockinette short-rows.

Finished Size

18" (45.5 cm) tall at center point and 51" (129.5 cm) wide.

Yarn

Lorna's Laces Helen's Lace (50% silk, 50% wool; 1,250 yd [1,143 m]/4 oz [113 g]): #512 cermak, 1 skein.

Needles

Size 6 (4 mm): 32" (81.5 cm) circular (cir); size 7 (4.5 mm): 1 needle for bind-off. *Adjust needle sizes if necessary to obtain the correct gauge.*

Notions

75 magatama drop beads 4×7mm; size 14 (.75 mm) crochet hook for bead placement; tapestry needle; blocking pins.

Gauge

19 sts and 28 rows = 4" (10 cm) in St st on smaller needles.

Shawl

With smaller needle, CO 21 sts.

NEXT ROW: (WS) Purl. Work Rows 1–18 of Mermaid's Song chart 25 times.

NEXT ROW: (RS) Knit. BO all sts pwise. Break yarn. With RS of border facing, join yarn at CO edge and pick up and knit 229 sts along straight edge of border as foll: Pick up and knit 1 st from CO edge st, pick up and knit 1 st from next row st, pick up and knit 1 st in each of next 225 sl sts, pick up and knit 1 st from next row st, pick up and knit 1 st from BO edge st. Inc row (WS) P7, *yo, p5; rep from * to last 7 sts, yo, p7—273 sts. Knit 1 RS row. Purl 1 WS row. Shape shawl with short-rows as foll:

SHORT-ROW 1: (RS) K140, turn.

SHORT-ROW 2: (WS) P7, turn.

SHORT-ROW 3: K6, ssk, k3, turn.

SHORT-ROW 4: P9, p2tog, p3, turn.

SHORT-ROW 5: K12, ssk, k3, turn.

SHORT-ROW 6: P15, p2tog, p3, turn.

SHORT-ROW 7: K18, ssk, k3, turn.

SHORT-ROW 8: P21, p2tog, p3, turn.

Rep last 2 short-rows 29 more times, working 3 additional sts before each turn, ending with a WS row.

NEXT SHORT-ROW: (RS) K198, ssk, k4, turn.

NEXT SHORT-ROW: (WS) P201, p2tog, p4, turn—all sts have been worked.

NEXT ROW: (RS) Purl.

NEXT ROW: (WS) Knit.

NEXT ROW: (RS) K1, *yo, k2tog; rep from * to end.

NEXT ROW: (WS) Knit. With larger needle, BO all sts as foll: *P2tog, return st to left needle; rep from * to end. Break yarn and pull through rem st.

Finishing

Weave in ends. Block piece to measurements, pinning out the points along edge. 🦎

SUSANNA IC lives in San Antonio, Texas, where she always looks for magic in the ordinary. Her projects and designs can be found on Ravelry, user name zuzusus, and at ArtQualia.com.

Mermaid's Song

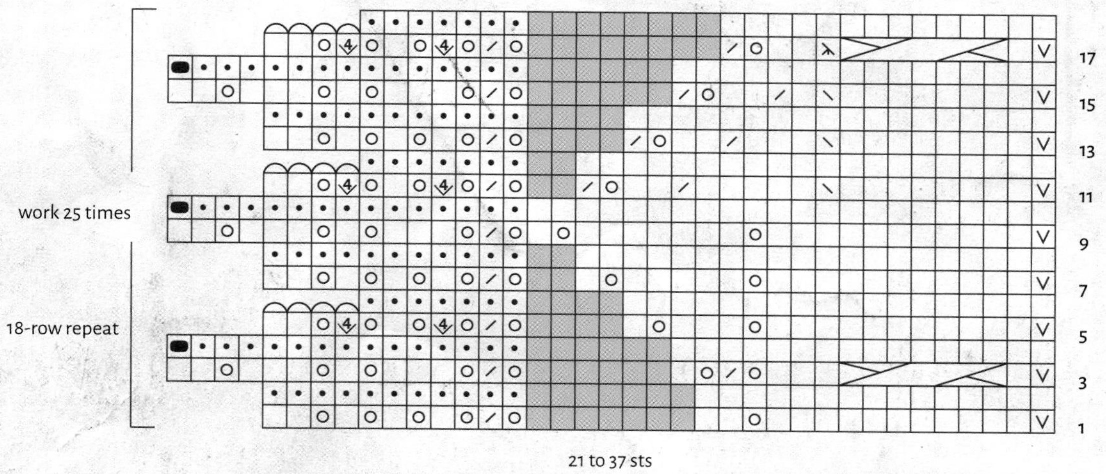

work 25 times
18-row repeat
17
15
13
11
9
7
5
3
1
21 to 37 sts

- k on RS; p on WS
- p on RS; k on WS
- sl 1 wyb
- yo
- k2tog
- ssk
- sssk (see Glossary)
- sl 1, k4tog, psso—4 sts dec'd
- bind off 1 st
- no stitch
- place bead: Slide bead onto crochet hook, insert crochet hook pwise into st and sl st onto crochet hook, slide bead down hook onto st, then return st to left needle and k1
- sl 3 sts onto cn, hold in back, k4, k3 from cn

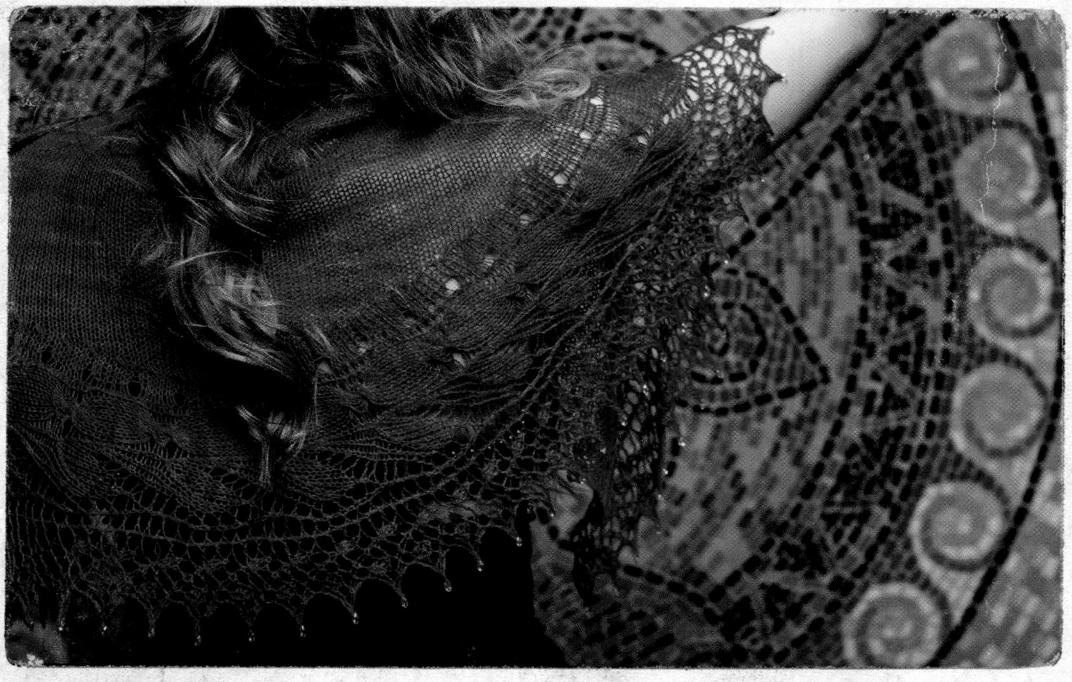

Owl Cardigan

⊰ Mari Chiba

*I*t takes a lot of wool to keep away the damp chill of the Northern winters and especially in a drafty old castle. For protection from more than the cold, owls' eyes peer out from the back and look for any mischief. The small pockets in the front are mostly decorative but could be used to hold something small and important, such as a skeleton key.

Finished Size

28¼ (32¼, 36¼, 40¼, 44¼, 48¼, 52¼)" (72 [82, 92, 102, 112.5, 122.5, 132.5] cm) bust circumference, buttoned. Cardigan shown measures 32¼" (82 cm).

Yarn

Classic Elite Yarns Woodland (65% wool, 35% nettles; 131 yd [119 m]/1¾ oz [50 g]): #3148 Prussian blue, 7 (7, 8, 9, 10, 11, 13) skeins.

Needles

Body and Sleeves—size 6 (4 mm): 32" (81.5 cm) circular (cir) and double-pointed (dpn).
Ribbing—size 4 (3.5 mm): 32" (81.5 cm) cir and dpn. *Adjust needle sizes if necessary to obtain the correct gauge.*

Notions

Markers (m); stitch holders; tapestry needle; eight 1" (2.5 cm) buttons.

Gauge

20 sts and 26 rows = 4" (10 cm) in St st on larger needles.

NOTES

✳ This cardigan is knitted from the bottom up in one piece. The body is worked from the bottom up, then the sleeves are worked in the round from the cuff, then body and sleeves are joined and knitted to the neck. The buttonband is picked up and knitted afterward.

✳ The number of stitches in the Owl pattern changes each row. Stitch counts will be given for front panels and the number of stitches on either side of the Owl chart.

Owl

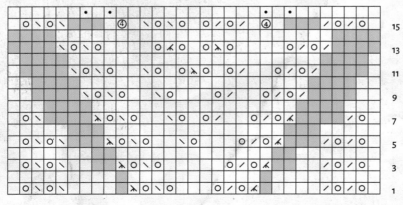

23 to 31 sts

☐		k on RS; p on WS
•		p on RS; k on WS
○		yo
╱		k2tog
╲		ssk
⼻		k3tog
⼼		sssk (see Glossary)
④		wrap yarn 4 times around needle
▨		no stitch

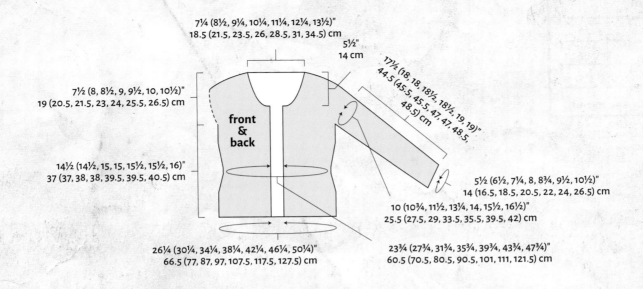

7¼ (8½, 9¼, 10¼, 11¼, 12¼, 13½)"
18.5 (21.5, 23.5, 26, 28.5, 31, 34.5) cm

5½"
14 cm

17½ (18, 18, 18½, 18½, 19, 19)"
44.5 (45.5, 45.5, 47, 47, 48.5, 48.5) cm

7½ (8, 8½, 9, 9½, 10, 10½)"
19 (20.5, 21.5, 23, 24, 25.5, 26.5) cm

front & back

14½ (14½, 15, 15, 15½, 15½, 16)"
37 (37, 38, 38, 39.5, 39.5, 40.5) cm

5½ (6½, 7¼, 8, 8¾, 9½, 10½)"
14 (16.5, 18.5, 20.5, 22, 24, 26.5) cm

10 (10¾, 11½, 13¼, 14, 15½, 16½)"
25.5 (27.5, 29, 33.5, 35.5, 39.5, 42) cm

26¼ (30¼, 34¼, 38¼, 42¼, 46¼, 50¼)"
66.5 (77, 87, 97, 107.5, 117.5, 127.5) cm

23¾ (27¾, 31¾, 35¾, 39¾, 43¾, 47¾)"
60.5 (70.5, 80.5, 90.5, 101, 111, 121.5) cm

Body

With smaller cir needle, CO 132 (152, 172, 192, 212, 232, 252) sts.

ROW 1: (WS) K1, *p2, k2; rep from * to last 3 sts, p3.

ROW 2: (RS) K1, *k2, p2; rep from * to last 3 sts, k3.

Rep Rows 1 and 2 until piece measures 4" (10 cm), ending with a WS row. Change to larger cir needle.

SET-UP ROW: (RS) K31 (36, 41, 46, 51, 56, 61), place marker (pm), k19 (24, 29, 34, 39, 44, 49), pm, k15, k2tog, k15, pm, k19 (24, 29, 34, 39, 44, 49), pm, k31 (36, 41, 46, 51, 56, 61) sts—131 (151, 171, 191, 211, 231, 251) sts rem.

NEXT ROW: (WS) K1, purl to last st, k1.

DEC ROW: (RS) Knit to 3 sts before m, ssk, k1, sl m, k1, k2tog, knit to next m, sl m, work Owl chart over 31 sts, sl m, knit to 3 sts before m, ssk, k1, sl m, k1, k2tog, knit to end—4 sts dec'd. Rep Dec Row every 8th row 2 more times—28 (33, 38, 43, 48, 53, 58) sts rem each front; 16 (21, 26, 31, 36, 41, 46) sts rem each back side panel on either side of Owl chart. Work 7 (7, 9, 9, 7, 9, 9) rows even in patt, ending with a WS row.

INC ROW: (RS) Knit to 1 st before m, M1R, k1, sl m, k1, M1L, knit to m, sl m, work charted patt as established to m, sl m, knit to 1 st before m, M1R, k1, sl m, k1, M1L, knit to end—4 sts inc'd. Rep Inc Row every 8th row 2 more times—31 (36, 41, 46, 51, 56, 61) sts each front; 19 (24, 29, 34, 39, 44, 49) sts each back side

panel on either side of Owl chart. Work even in patt until piece measures 11½ (11½, 12, 12, 12½, 12½, 13)" (29 [29, 30.5, 30.5, 31.5, 31.5, 33] cm) from CO edge, ending with a WS row.

Shape Bust

Shape bust with short-rows as foll:

Note: *The number of short-rows will depend on your bra cup size, not the garment size.*

A cup
Work 0 additional short-rows.

B cup
Work 3 additional short-rows.

C cup
Work 6 additional short-rows.

D cup
Work 9 additional short-rows.

DD cup
Work 12 additional short-rows.

Short-rows for each side of the cardigan are worked separately as foll:

Right Front Bust Shaping

SHORT-ROW 1: (RS) Knit to 2 sts before m, wrap next st, turn.

SHORT-ROW 2: (WS) Purl to last st, k1.

SHORT-ROW 3: (RS) Knit to 3 sts before last wrapped st, wrap next st, turn.

SHORT-ROW 4: (WS) Purl to last st, k1. Rep last 2 Short-rows the number of times needed for your bra cup size.

NEXT ROW: (RS) Work in patt to end, working wraps tog with wrapped sts as you come to them.

Left Front Bust Shaping

SHORT-ROW 1: (WS) K1, purl to 2 before m, wrap next st, turn.

SHORT-ROW 2: (RS) Knit.

SHORT-ROW 3: (WS) K1, purl to 3 sts before last wrapped st, wrap next st, turn.

SHORT-ROW 4: (RS) Knit. Rep last 2 Short-rows the number of times needed for your bra cup size.

NEXT ROW: (WS) K1, purl to last st, k1, working wraps tog with wrapped sts as you come to them. Work even in patt until back measures 14½ (14½, 15, 15, 15½, 15½, 16)" (37 [37, 38, 38, 39.5, 39.5, 40.5] cm) from CO edge, ending with a WS row. Break yarn.

Sleeves

With smaller dpn, CO 28 (32, 36, 40, 44, 48, 52) sts. Pm and join in the rnd.

NEXT RND: *P2, k2; rep from * to end. Work in rib as established until piece measures 4" (10 cm). Change to larger dpn. Knit 1 rnd.

INC RND: K1, M1L, knit to last st, M1R, k1—2 sts inc'd. Rep Inc Rnd every 7 (7, 7, 6, 6, 6, 6)th rnd 10 (10, 10, 12, 12, 14, 14) more times—50 (54, 58, 66, 70, 78, 82) sts. Work even in St st until sleeve measures 17½ (18, 18, 18½, 18½, 19, 19)" (44.5 [45.5, 45.5, 47, 47, 48.5, 48.5] cm) from CO edge.

NEXT RND: Knit to last 6 (6, 7, 8, 9, 10, 10) sts, place next 12 (12, 14, 16, 18, 20, 20) sts on holder for underarm—38 (42, 44, 50, 52, 58, 62) sleeve sts rem.

Yoke

JOINING ROW: (RS) With RS facing, knit front sts to 6 (6, 7, 8, 9, 10, 10) sts before m, place next 12 (12, 14, 16, 18, 20, 20) sts on holder for underarm, removing m, k38 (42, 44, 50, 52, 58, 62) sleeve sts, knit to m, sl m, work charted patt as established to m, sl m, knit to 6 (6, 7, 8, 9, 10, 10) sts before m, place next 12 (12, 14, 16, 18, 20, 20) sts on holder for underarm, removing m, k38 (42, 44, 50, 52, 58, 62) sleeve sts, knit to end—76 (90, 100, 114, 124, 138, 152) sts each side of m; 25 (30, 34, 38, 42, 46, 51) sts each front; 38 (42, 44, 50, 52, 58, 62) sts each sleeve; 13 (18, 22, 26, 30, 34, 39) sts each back side panel on either side of Owl chart.

NEXT ROW: (WS) K1, purl to m, sl m, work charted patt as established to m, sl m, purl to last st, k1.

NEXT ROW: (RS) K1, knit to m, sl m, work charted patt as established to m, sl m, knit to end.

Rep last 2 rows until piece measures 2 (2½, 3, 3½, 4, 4½, 5)" (5 [6.5, 7.5, 9, 10, 11.5, 12.5] cm) from underarm, ending with a WS row.

DEC ROW: (RS) K1, ssk, k3 (2, 2, 1, 1, 0, 4), *ssk, k3; rep from * to m, sl m, work charted patt as established to m, sl m, k3 (2, 2, 1, 1, 0, 4), *k2tog, k3; rep from * to last 3 sts, k2tog, k1—61 (72, 80, 91, 99, 110, 122) sts rem each side of m.

NEXT ROW: (WS) K1, purl to m, sl m, work charted patt as established to m, sl m, purl to last st, k1.

DEC ROW: (RS) K1, ssk, knit to m, sl m, work charted patt as established to m, sl m, knit to last 3 sts, k2tog, k1—2 sts dec'd. Rep last 2 rows 5 more times—55 (66, 74, 85, 93, 104, 116) sts rem each side of m.

DEC ROW: (RS) K1, ssk, k0 (3, 3, 2, 2, 1, 1), *ssk, k2; rep from * to m, sl m, work charted patt as established to m, sl m, k0 (3, 3, 2, 2, 1, 1), *k2tog, k2; rep from * to last 3 sts, k2tog, k1—41 (50, 56, 64, 70, 78, 87) sts rem each side of m.

NEXT ROW: (WS) K1, purl to m, sl m, work charted patt as established to m, sl m, purl to last st, k1.

DEC ROW: (RS) K1, ssk, knit to m, sl m, work charted patt as established to m, sl m, knit to last 3 sts, k2tog, k1—2 sts dec'd. Rep last 2 rows 4 more times—36 (45, 51, 59, 65, 73, 82) sts rem each side of m.

DEC ROW: (RS) K1, ssk, k0 (0, 0, 2, 2, 1, 1), *ssk, k1; rep from * to m, sl m, work charted patt as established to m, sl m, k0 (0, 0, 2, 2, 1, 1), *k2tog, k1; rep from * to last 3 sts, k2tog, k1—24 (30, 34, 40, 44, 49, 55) sts rem each side of m.

NEXT ROW: (WS) K1, purl to m, sl m, work charted patt as established to m, sl m, purl to last st, k1.

DEC ROW: (RS) K1, ssk, knit to m, sl m, work charted patt as established to m, sl m, knit to last 3 sts, k2tog, k1—2 sts dec'd. Rep last 2 rows 3 more times—36 (45, 51, 59, 65, 73, 82) sts rem each side of m.

DEC ROW: (RS) *Ssk; rep from * to center st of Owl chart, *k2tog; rep from * to end—the number of sts will vary depending on which row of the Owl chart you knit last.

If you just completed Row 1—35 (41, 45, 51, 55, 60, 66) sts rem.

If you just completed Row 3—34 (40, 44, 50, 54, 59, 65) sts rem.

If you just completed Row 5—33 (39, 43, 49, 53, 58, 64) sts rem.

If you just completed Rows 7, 9, 11 or 13—32 (38, 42, 48, 52, 57, 63) sts rem.

If you just completed Row 15—36 (42, 46, 52, 56, 61, 67) sts rem.

Break yarn and place all rem sts on holder.

Finishing
Frontbands

Note: Pick up and knit a multiple of 4 sts plus 3 along each front edge. Make sure you pick up the same number of sts for each band.

Buttonband

With smaller cir needle and RS facing, pick up and knit 2 sts for every 3 rows along left front.

NEXT ROW: (WS) *P2, k2; rep from * to last 3 sts, p3. Work in rib patt as established for 2" (5 cm), ending with a WS row. BO all sts kwise.

Buttonhole band

With smaller cir needle and RS facing, pick up and knit 2 sts for every 3 rows along right front.

NEXT ROW: (WS) P3, *k2, p2; rep from * to end. Work in rib patt as established for 1" (2.5 cm), ending with a WS row. Mark 8 buttonholes evenly on the buttonband.

BUTTONHOLE ROW: (RS) *Work in patt to hole placement, k2tog, using the backward-loop method (see Glossary), CO 2 sts, ssk; rep from * 7 more times, work in patt to end. Work in patt until buttonhole band measures 2" (5 cm), ending with a WS row. BO all sts kwise.

Neck edging

With smaller cir needle, RS facing, and beg at right front, pick up and knit 2 sts for every 3 rows along the top of the button band and right front neck to back of neck sts, knit back neck sts from holder, pick up and knit 2 sts for every 3 rows along the left front neck and the top of left buttonband. Work in garter st (knit every row) for 6 rows. BO all sts.

Pockets (make 2)

With larger needle, CO 20 sts. Work in St st until piece measures 3" (7.5 cm). Work in garter st for 6 rows. BO all sts.

Weave in ends. Graft underarm sts. Block sweater to measurements. Sew pockets to fronts about ¾" (2 cm) above the bottom ribbing and ¾" (2 cm) from buttonband. Sew on buttons. 🦁

MARI CHIBA currently knits in Raleigh, North Carolina, and can be found on Ravelry as MariChiba and at mariknits.com.

Midnight *Mitts*

⊹ Elizabeth Cherry

*Y*ou'll need some lacy mitts to keep your hands warm as you sneak around the castle at night. These mitts are also functional, as they provide a handy place to hide your wand while you work your mischief. The asymmetrical lace panel, found in an old German lace book, and buttoned side panel give them a delicate elegance, perfect for your own wanderings on a chilly afternoon.

Finished Size
6¼ (7, 7¾)" (16 [18, 19.5] cm) hand circumference and 11¾" (30 cm) long. Shown in size 6¼" (16 cm).

Yarn
The Fibre Company Road to China Light (65% baby alpaca, 15% silk, 10% cashmere, 10% camel; 159 yd [145 m]/1¾ oz [50 g]): #691 abalone, 1 (2, 2) skeins. Yarn distibuted by Kelbourne Woolens.

Needles
Size 5 (3.75 mm): straight and set of double-pointed (dpn). *Adjust needle size if necessary to obtain the correct gauge.*

Notions
Markers (m); tapestry needle; twelve ½" (1.3 cm) buttons.

Gauge
24 sts and 32 rows = 4" (10 cm) in St st.

Right Mitt

With straight needles, CO 46 (50, 55) sts. Knit 1 row. Purl 1 row.

NEXT ROW: (RS) K1 (3, 1), *yo, k2, ssk, k2tog, k2, yo, k1; rep from * to last 0 (2, 0) sts, k0 (2, 0). Rep the last 2 rows 3 more times.

NEXT ROW: (WS) Purl, dec 0 (1, 0) st—46 (50, 54) sts.

BUTTONHOLE ROW: (RS) P2, k2tog, yo, place marker (pm), work Row 1 of Lace chart over 9 sts, pm, knit to end.

NEXT ROW: (WS) Purl to m, sl m, work Lace chart, sl m, p2, k2. Continue in patt for 6 more rows ending with a WS row.

BUTTONHOLE ROW: (RS) P2, k2tog, yo, sl m, work in patt to end. Work 7 rows even.

DEC ROW: (RS) P2, k2tog, yo, sl m, work Lace chart, sl m, k8 (10, 12), k2tog, knit to last 3 sts, ssk, k1—44 (48, 52) sts rem. Work 7 rows even.

DEC ROW: (RS) P2, k2tog, yo, sl m, work Lace chart, sl m, k7 (9, 11), k2tog, knit to last 3 sts, ssk, k1—42 (46, 50) sts rem. Work 7 rows even.

DEC ROW: (RS) P2, k2tog, yo, sl m, work Lace chart, sl m, k6 (8, 10), k2tog, knit to last 3 sts, ssk, k1—40 (44, 48) sts rem. Work 7 rows even.

Form Placket Overlap

(RS) Transfer sts to dpn. Sl 3 sts from right needle onto a spare needle. Hold spare needle behind left needle. [Knit 1 st from left needle tog with 1 st from spare needle] 3 times, k1, yo, sl m, work to end—38 (42, 46) sts rem.

Next rnd: K2, k2tog, pm for beg of rnd, work to end—37 (41, 45) sts rem. Work 6 rnds even.

Thumb Gusset

NEXT RND: Work 15 (17, 19) sts, pm for gusset, yo, pm, knit to end—38 (42, 46) sts. Work 1 rnd even.

INC RND: Work to gusset m, sl m, yo, knit to m, yo, sl m, knit to end—2 sts inc'd. Rep Inc Rnd on every other rnd 6 (6, 7) more times—52 (56, 62) sts. Work 1 rnd even.

NEXT RND: Work to gusset m, remove m, loosely BO 15 (15, 17) sts, removing m, knit to end—37 (41, 45) sts rem.

NEXT RND: Work to BO gap, use the backward-loop method (see Glossary) to CO 3 sts, knit to end—40 (44, 48) sts.

NEXT RND: Work to 1 st before CO sts, k2tog, k1, ssk, knit to end—38 (42, 46) sts rem. Work 8 (8, 6) rnds even. Purl 1 rnd. Knit 1 rnd. Purl 1 rnd. Loosely BO all sts.

Left Mitt

With straight needles, CO 46 (50, 55) sts. Knit 1 row. Purl 1 row.

NEXT ROW: (RS) K1 (3, 1), *yo, k2, ssk, k2tog, k2, yo, k1; rep from * to last 0 (2, 0) sts, k0 (2, 0). Rep the last 2 rows 3 more times.

NEXT ROW: (WS) Purl, dec 0 (0, 1) st—46 (50, 54) sts.

BUTTONHOLE ROW: (RS) K33 (37, 41), pm, work Row 1 of Lace chart over 9 sts, pm, yo, ssk, p2.

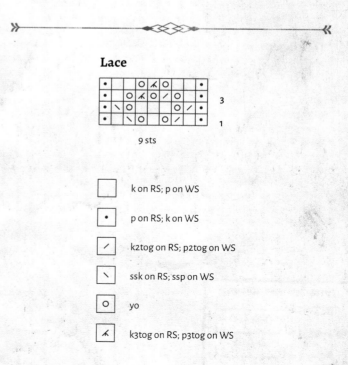

Lace

9 sts

•			O	⋏	O			•
•		O	⋏	O	/	O		•
•	\	O				O	/	•
	\	O				O	/	

3

1

☐ k on RS; p on WS

▪ p on RS; k on WS

╱ k2tog on RS; p2tog on WS

╲ ssk on RS; ssp on WS

O yo

⋏ k3tog on RS; p3tog on WS

Form Placket Overlap

(RS) Transfer sts to dpn. Sl 3 sts from right needle onto a spare needle. Hold spare needle in front of left needle. [Knit 1 st from spare needle tog with 1 st from left needle] 3 times, work to last st, yo, k2tog (last st of rnd tog with first st of rnd)—37 (41, 45) sts rem.

NEXT RND: K2, pm for beg of rnd, work to end. Work 6 rnds even.

Thumb Gusset

NEXT RND: K18 (20, 22), pm for gusset, yo, pm, work to end—38 (42, 46) sts. Work 1 rnd even.

INC RND: Knit to gusset m, sl m, yo, knit to m, yo, sl m, work to end—2 sts inc'd. Rep Inc Rnd on every other rnd 6 (6, 7) more times—52 (56, 62) sts. Work 1 rnd even.

NEXT RND: Knit to gusset m, remove m, loosely BO 15 (15, 17) sts, removing m, knit to end—37 (41, 45) sts rem.

NEXT RND: Knit to BO gap, use the backward-loop method to CO 3 sts, work to end—40 (44, 48) sts.

NEXT RND: Knit to 1 st before CO sts, k2tog, k1, ssk, work to end—38 (42, 46) sts rem. Work 8 (8, 6) rnds even. Purl 1 rnd. Knit 1 rnd. Purl 1 rnd. Loosely BO all sts.

Finishing

Weave in ends. Block. Sew on buttons.

ELIZABETH CHERRY is a seamstress, milliner, and knitter for theater in New York City, whose work can be seen on Broadway, on national tours, as well as in the occasional dance and opera company. She also spins and teaches knitting for Maupston Design Studio, a New York–based fiber company that sells to private clients as well as at several farmer's markets throughout the New York State area. Read her blog at drowninginpretty.blogspot.com.

NEXT ROW: (WS) K2, p2, sl m, work Lace chart, sl m, purl to end. Continue in patt for 6 more rows ending with a WS row.

BUTTONHOLE ROW: (RS) Work to last 4 sts, sl m, yo, ssk, p2. Work 7 rows even.

DEC ROW: (RS) K1, k2tog, knit to 9 (11, 13) sts before m, ssk, work to last 4 sts, sl m, yo, ssk, p2—44 (48, 52) sts rem. Work 7 rows even.

DEC ROW: (RS) K1, k2tog, knit to 8 (10, 12) sts before m, ssk, work to last 4 sts, sl m, yo, ssk, p2—42 (46, 50) sts rem. Work 7 rows even.

DEC ROW: (RS) K1, k2tog, knit to 7 (9, 11) sts before m, ssk, work to last 4 sts, sl m, yo, ssk, p2—40 (44, 48) sts rem. Work 7 rows even.

Rendez-vous *Mitts*

⚜ Sherri Sulkowski

When arranging a meetup with even the most intuitive of creatures (magical or mundane), it helps to carry an identifying mark, especially if you leave your wizard's cloak at home in favor of a less-attention-grabbing wool coat. The initial marking these mitts will ensure that when you see your intended buddy, he or she will know that it's you.

Finished Size

5½ (6, 6½)" (14 [15, 16.5] cm) wrist circumference, unstretched. Mittens shown measure 6" (15 cm).

Yarn

Swans Island Fingering (100% organic Merino; 525 yd [480 m]/3½ oz [100 g]): #118 logwood (MC), 1 skein; #101 garnet (CC), 1 skein.

Needles

Size 3 (3.25 mm): set of double-pointed needles (dpn). Adjust needle size if necessary to obtain correct gauge.

Notions

Size 6 (1.8 mm) steel crochet hook; markers (m); stitch holder; cable needle (cn); tapestry needle.

Gauge

44 sts and 47 rows = 4" (10 cm) in Cable patt, relaxed.

Stitch Guide

CROCHET CO: With crochet hook and CC, ch the number of sts needed for CO. Fasten off. With dpn and MC, pick up and knit 1 st in each bump along back of crochet ch.

Left Mitt

Cuff

Using crochet CO (see Stitch Guide), CO 60 (66, 72) sts. Place marker (pm) and join in the rnd. Work Rnds 1–6 of Left Cable chart 6 times.

Thumb Gusset

NEXT RND: Work 6 sts in patt, pm, work Rnd 1 of Left Initial chart over 18 sts, pm, work in patt to last 20 sts, [p1, k1f&b, work 4 sts in patt] 3 times, k1f&b, p1—64 (70, 76) sts.

NEXT RND: Work in patt to last 24 sts, [p3, work 4 sts in patt] 3 times, p3.

NEXT RND: Work in patt to last 24 sts, [p2, k1f&b, work 4 sts in patt] 3 times, k1f&b, p2—68 (74, 80) sts.

NEXT RND: Work in patt to last 28 sts, [p4, work 4 sts in patt] 3 times, p4. Continue in patt until Left Initial chart is complete, ending with Rnd 6 of Left Cable chart.

NEXT RND: Work to m, remove m, work Rnd 1 of Left Cable chart over 18 sts, remove m, work in patt to end. Continue in patt until mitt measures about 6" (15 cm) from CO, ending with Rnd 6 of chart.

Next rnd: Work in patt to last 26 sts, place next 24 sts on holder for thumb, use the knitted CO (see Glossary) to CO 4 sts, work to end—48 (54, 60) sts.

Hand

Work next rnd of Left Cable chart over all sts. Continue in patt until mitt measures about 7¼" (18.5 cm) from CO, ending with Rnd 4 of chart. Using CC, BO all sts kwise.

Left Cable

6 st repeat

Right Cable

6 st repeat

Left Initial

18 sts

Right Initial

18 sts

* See page 39 for full alphabet chart

☐	k
•	p
✛	duplicate st with CC
☐	pattern repeat

sl 1 st onto cn, hold in back, k2, k1 from cn
sl 2 sts onto cn, hold in front, k1, k2 from cn
sl 2 sts onto cn, hold in back, k2, k2 from cn
sl 2 sts onto cn, hold in front, k2, k2 from cn

Thumb

Place 24 sts from holder onto needles. Join MC, pick up and knit 8 sts across CO edge, work in established cable patt over 24 sts, pm for beg of rnd—32 sts.

NEXT RND: P2, k4, [p2, p2tog, work 4 sts in patt] 3 times, p2tog—28 sts. Work 1 rnd even.

NEXT RND: P2tog, work 4 sts in patt, [p1, p2tog, work 4 sts in patt] 3 times, p1—24 sts. Work 7 rnds even. Using CC, BO all sts kwise.

Right Mitt
Cuff

Using crochet CO (see Stitch Guide), CO 60 (66, 72) sts. Pm and join in the rnd. Work Rnds 1–6 of Right Cable chart 6 times.

Thumb Gusset

NEXT RND: [P1, k1f&b, work 4 sts in patt] 3 times, k1f&b, p1, work in patt to last 24 sts, pm, work Rnd 1 of Right Initial chart over 18 sts, pm, work 6 sts in patt—64 (70, 76) sts.

NEXT RND: [P3, work 4 sts in patt] 3 times, p3, work in patt to end.

NEXT RND: [P2, k1f&b, work 4 sts in patt] 3 times, k1f&b, p2, work in patt to end—68 (74, 80) sts.

NEXT RND: [P4, work 4 sts in patt] 3 times, p4, work in patt to end. Continue in patt until Right Initial chart is complete, ending with Rnd 6 of Right Cable chart.

NEXT RND: Work in established patt to m, remove m, work Rnd 1 of Right Cable chart over 18 sts, remove m, work to end. Continue in patt until mitt measures about 6" (15 cm) from CO, ending with Rnd 6 of chart.

NEXT RND: Work 2 sts in patt, place next 24 sts on holder for thumb, use the knitted CO to CO 4 sts, work to end—48 (54, 60) sts.

Hand

Work next rnd of Right Cable chart over all sts. Continue in patt until mitt measures about 7¼" (18.5 cm) from CO, ending with Rnd 4 of chart. Using CC, BO all sts kwise. Work thumb as for left mitt.

Finishing

Weave in ends. Work monogram in duplicate st, following chart. See page 39 for full alphabet chart. 🦁

SHERRI SULKOWSKI lives in southwestern Pennsylvania with her husband, James (an artist), and a greyhound named Grace. She has knitted since childhood and has taught knitting since 1992, including to her favorite students—children. In addition to being the mother of two grown children, she has worked at a local yarn shop, a felted handbag company, and has hosted KnitOn! (a knitting show on a local community television station). Now she works as a wine consultant.

Blue Moon *Shawl*

❧ Hannah Poon

Once in a blue moon, you can push the spell books aside and wrap yourself up in the loving waves of this shawl and take a stroll at midnight. You never know whom you might bump into.

Finished Size

14" (35.5 cm) wide and 63" (160 cm) long, excluding edging.

Yarn

Manos del Uruguay Silk Blend (70% Merino, 30% silk; 150 yd [137 m]/1¾ oz [50 g]): #3043 juniper, 6 skeins.

Yarn distributed by Fairmount Fibers.

Needles

Size 6 (4 mm). *Adjust needle size if necessary to obtain the correct gauge.*

Notions

Tapestry needle.

Gauge

24 sts and 32 rows = 4" (10 cm) in St st.

Stitch Guide

Sk2p: Sl 1 kwise, k2tog, psso—2 sts dec'd.

> ### NOTE
> ❋ *K1f&b can be replaced with k1, M1R. K1b&f can be replaced with M1L, k1. The slightly different look of these stitches will affect the edges of the work, so use one or the other throughout for consistency.*

Shawl

CO 55 sts.

Base Triangle

ROW 1: (WS) Sl 1, p1, turn.

ROW 2: K2, turn.

ROW 3: Sl 1, p2, turn.

ROW 4: K3, turn.

ROW 5: Sl 1, p3, turn.

ROW 6: K4, turn.

ROW 7: Sl 1, p4, turn.

ROW 8: K5, turn.

ROW 9: Sl 1, p5, turn.

ROW 10: K6, turn.

ROW 11: Sl 1, p6, turn.

ROW 12: K7, turn.

ROW 13: Sl 1, p7, turn.

ROW 14: K8, turn.

ROW 15: Sl 1, p8, turn.

ROW 16: K9, turn.

ROW 17: Sl 1, p9, turn.

ROW 18: K10, turn.

ROW 19: Sl 1, p10, do not turn.

Rep Rows 1–19 four more times—5 base triangles.

Tier 1

Right Side Triangle

ROW 1: (RS) K2, turn.

ROW 2: P2, turn.

ROW 3: K1f&b, ssk, turn.

ROW 4: P3, turn.

ROW 5: K1f&b, k1, ssk, turn.

ROW 6: P4, turn.

ROW 7: K1f&b, k2, ssk, turn.

ROW 8: P5, turn.

ROW 9: K1f&b, k3, ssk, turn.

ROW 10: P6, turn.

ROW 11: K1f&b, k4, ssk, turn.

ROW 12: P7, turn.

ROW 13: K1f&b, k5, ssk, turn.

ROW 14: P8, turn.

ROW 15: K1f&b, k6, ssk, turn.

ROW 16: P9, turn.

ROW 17: K1f&b, k7, ssk, turn.

ROW 18: P10, turn.

ROW 19: K1f&b, k8, ssk, do not turn.

Left-Slanting Flame Rectangle

With RS facing, pick up and knit 11 sts along left side of triangle or rectangle from previous row, turn.

ROW 1 AND ALL WS ROWS: P11, turn.

ROW 2: K3, k2tog, yo, k1, yo, ssk, k2, ssk, turn.

ROW 4: K2, k2tog, [k1, yo] 2 times, [k1, ssk] 2 times, turn.

ROW 6: K1, k2tog, k2, yo, k1, yo, k2, [ssk] 2 times, turn.

ROW 8: K1f&b, ssk, k5, k2tog, M1L, ssk, turn.

ROW 10: K1f&b, k1, ssk, k3, k2tog, k1, M1L, ssk, turn.

ROW 12: K1f&b, k2, ssk, k1, k2tog, k2, M1L, ssk, turn.

ROW 14: K1f&b, k3, sk2p (see Stitch Guide), k3, M1L, ssk, turn.

ROWS 16, 18, AND 20: K10, ssk, turn.

ROW 22: K10, ssk, do not turn; do not work a WS row.

Work 3 more left-slanting flame rectangles.

Left Side Triangle

With RS facing, pick up and knit 11 sts along left side of triangle or rectangle from previous row, turn.

ROW 1: (WS) P2tog, p9, turn.

ROW 2: K10, turn.

ROW 3: P2tog, p8, turn.

ROW 4: K9, turn.

ROW 5: P2tog, p7, turn.

ROW 6: K8, turn.

ROW 7: P2tog, p6, turn.

ROW 8: K7, turn.

ROW 9: P2tog, p5, turn.

ROW 10: K6, turn.

ROW 11: P2tog, p4, turn.

ROW 12: K5, turn.

ROW 13: P2tog, p3, turn.

ROW 14: K4, turn.

ROW 15: P2tog, p2, turn.

ROW 16: K3, turn.

ROW 17: P2tog, p1, turn.

ROW 18: K2, turn.

ROW 19: P2tog, do not turn.

Tier 2:

Right-Slanting Flame Rectangle

With WS facing, pick up and purl 10 sts along side of triangle or rectangle from previous row, turn—11 sts for rectangle.

ROW 1: (RS) K3, k2tog, yo, k1, yo, ssk, k3, turn.

ROW 2 AND ALL WS ROWS: P10, p2tog, turn.

ROW 3: K2, k2tog, [k1, yo] 2 times, k1, ssk, k2, turn.

ROW 5: K1, k2tog, k2, yo, k1, yo, k2, ssk, k1, turn.

ROW 7: K1, M1R, ssk, k5, k2tog, k1b&f, turn.

ROW 9: K1, M1R, k1, ssk, k3, k2tog, k1, k1b&f, turn.

ROW 11: K1, M1R, k2, ssk, k1, k2tog, k2, k1b&f, turn.

ROW 13: K1, M1R, k3, sk2p, k3, k1b&f, turn.

ROWS 15, 17, 19, AND 21: K11, turn.

ROW 22: P10, p2tog, do not turn.

Work 4 more right-slanting flame rectangles, picking up and purling 11 sts rather than 10.

Tiers 3–35

[Work tier 1, then tier 2] 16 times, then work tier 1 once more.

Ending Triangle

With WS facing, pick up and purl 9 sts along triangle or rectangle from previous row, then pick up and purl 1 st tog with first st from next rectangle or triangle, turn—11 sts for triangle.

ROW 1: (RS) K11, turn.

ROW 2: P2tog, p8, p2tog, turn.

ROW 3: K10, turn.

ROW 4: P2tog, p7, p2tog, turn.

ROW 5: K9, turn.

ROW 6: P2tog, p6, p2tog, turn.

ROW 7: K8, turn.

ROW 8: P2tog, p5, p2tog, turn.

ROW 9: K7, turn.

ROW 10: P2tog, p4, p2tog, turn.

ROW 11: K6, turn.

ROW 12: P2tog, p3, p2tog, turn.

ROW 13: K5, turn.

ROW 14: P2tog, p2, p2tog, turn.

ROW 15: K4, turn.

ROW 16: P2tog, p1, p2tog, turn.

ROW 17: K3, turn.

ROW 18: [P2tog] 2 times, turn.

ROW 19: K2, turn.

ROW 20: Sl 1, p2tog, turn.

ROW 21: K2, turn.

ROW 22: P2tog, do not turn.

Work 4 more ending triangles. Fasten off last st.

Finishing

Weave in loose ends.

Edging

With RS facing, pick up and knit 7 sts along a base triangle, centering sts on triangle.

ROW 1 AND ALL WS ROWS: Purl.

ROW 2: K1, k2tog, yo, k1, yo, ssk, k1.

ROW 4: K2tog, k1, yo, k1, yo, k1, ssk.

ROW 6: Ssk, k3, k2tog—5 sts rem.

ROW 8: Ssk, k1, k2tog—3 sts rem.

ROW 10: Sk2p—1 st rem.

Break yarn, leaving a 6" (15 cm) tail. Fasten off last st. Cut a 12" (30.5 cm) length of yarn and pull halfway through top of point just worked. Braid (see Glossary) 3 strands tog and finish with an overhand knot 2" (5 cm) from end. Rep for all base and ending triangles. ✦

HANNAH POON lives and knits in Ontario, Canada, where the many varied seasons provide plenty of inspiration for cozy knits. When she is not knitting, she is running after a toddler or enjoying time with her husband of eight years—she has long since given up the pastime of attempting to keep a tidy home. Hannah is a knitter, a spinner, a weaver, and a designer, and owns and operates Mousewife on Etsy. She is a big fan of science fiction and fantasy and enjoys soaking away the troubles of her day in a bubble bath with a good book—any good book will do.

Cotillion
Arm Warmers

❧ *Corrina Ferguson*

These fancy gloves would complement a lovely ball gown for an enchanted event. They combine classic feather-and-fan patterning with seed stitch and just a smidge of crochet to make up gloves suitable for any dress-up occasion. And with all the rich Tosh Sock colors to choose from, you can't go wrong.

Finished Size

6¼ (6½, 7½)" (16 [16.5, 19] cm) wrist circumference, 8½ (9½, 10¼)" (21.5 [24, 26] cm) upper arm circumference, and 17 (18½, 19½)" (43 [47, 49.5] cm) long from cuff to tip. Glove shown measures 6¼" (16 cm) at wrist.

Yarn

Madelinetosh Tosh Sock (100% superwash Merino; 395 yd [361 m]/3½ oz [100 g]): clematis, 1 skein.

Needles

Size 6 (4 mm): set of double-pointed (dpn). *Adjust needle size if necessary to obtain the correct gauge.*

Notions

Markers (m); tapestry needle; size E/4 (3.5 mm) crochet hook.

Gauge

28 sts and 32 rows = 4" (10 cm) in St st. 21 st Lace = 3" (7.5 cm) wide.

Cuff

Using the provisional CO method (see Glossary), CO 12 sts. Work
Rows 1–8 of Cuff chart 10 (11, 12) times. Cut yarn, leaving a 12"
(30.5 cm) tail. Place 12 sts from provisional CO onto a second
needle. Use Kitchener st (see Glossary) and yarn tail to graft CO
sts tog with last row of live sts.

Sleeve

Beg at grafted seam, with RS facing, pick up and knit 60 (66,
72) sts from straight edge of cuff. Place marker (pm) for beg
of rnd. Purl 1 rnd.

SET-UP RND: K9 (12, 15), pm, work Rnd 1 (11, 1) of Lace chart over
21 sts, pm, k9 (12, 15), pm, work Rnd 1 (11, 1) of Lace chart over
21 sts. Continue in patt, work 19 (9, 19) rnds even, ending with
Rnd 20 of chart.

DEC RND: *Ssk, knit to 2 sts before m, k2tog, sl m, work next
rnd of chart, sl m; rep from * once more—4 sts dec'd. Work 19
rnds even. Rep the last 20 rows 3 (4, 4) more times—44 (46,
52) sts rem.

Shape Point

NEXT RND: Loosely BO 23 (25, 31) sts, work Row 1 of Hand Point
chart—19 sts rem. Working back and forth, work Rows 2–18 of
chart—1 st rem. Do not fasten off and do not cut yarn.

Finishing

Using crochet hook and beg with rem st at point of glove,
ch 12 (14, 16), or long enough to loop comfortably around
the middle finger. Join end of ch to point with sl st. With RS
facing, work 1 row of sc along each side of hand point. Weave
in ends. Block. 🐉

CORRINA FERGUSON knits and designs in Florida where there are
only about three sweater days per year. But she keeps on knitting anyway
and dreams of someday retiring somewhere where it snows.

Lace

21 sts

Hand Point

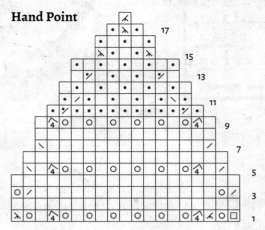

21 sts dec'd to 1 st

Cuff

12 sts

	k on RS; p on WS
•	p on RS; k on WS
╱	k2tog
╲	ssk
⊬	p2tog on RS; k2tog on WS
⋌	k3tog on RS; p3tog on WS
⋋	sl 1, k2tog, psso
⋏	k4tog
⋀	sl 1, k3tog, psso
O	yo
▢	st on needle after BO
⌒	bind off 1 st

Inky Pullover

⁜ Josie Mercier

Wizards don't often wear robes to their day jobs, so how to project the appropriate aura of menace in street clothes? The Inky Pullover features a central column of offset cables reminiscent of flickering flames, flanked by narrow, serpentine cables. The sleeves feature the same serpentine cable that travels the length of the sleeve and forms a saddle shoulder.

Finished Size

32 (38½, 42½, 46½, 50)" (81.5 [98, 108, 118, 127] cm) chest circumference. Pullover shown measures 42½" (108 cm).

Yarn

Patons Classic Wool Worsted (100% wool; 210 yd [192 m]/3½ oz [100 g]): #77044 mercury, 8 (9, 10, 11, 12) skeins.

Needles

Body and sleeves—size 7 (4.5 mm): 24" (61 cm) circular (cir). Ribbing—size 6 (4 mm): 16" (40.5 cm) and 24" (61 cm) cir. *Adjust needle size if necessary to obtain the correct gauge.*

Notions

Markers (m); stitch holders; cable needle (cn); tapestry needle.

Gauge

20 sts and 26 rows = 4" (10 cm) in rev St st on larger needle; 24 sts of Center Cable patt = 3½" (9 cm) wide.

Back

With smaller needle, CO 106 (128, 144, 154, 168) sts. Do not join. Work in k1, p1 rib until piece measures 1½" (3.8 cm) from CO, ending with a WS row. Change to larger needle.

NEXT ROW: (RS) P6 (6, 3, 8, 4), [work Row 1 of Right Cable chart, p2] 1 (2, 3, 3, 4) time(s), work Row 1 of Center Cable chart over 24 sts, work Row 13 of Center Cable chart over 24 sts, work Row 1 of Center Cable chart over 24 sts, [p2, work Row 1 of Left Cable chart] 1 (2, 3, 3, 4) time(s), p6 (6, 3, 8, 4). Work even in patt until piece measures 15½ (16¼, 16¼, 16¾, 17)" (39.5 [41.5, 41.5, 42.5, 43] cm) from CO, or desired length to underarm, ending with a RS row.

Shape Armholes

BO 3 (4, 5, 6, 7) sts at beg of next 2 rows—100 (120, 134, 142, 154) sts rem.

NOTES

✳ This sweater is worked flat in pieces from the bottom up. The sleeves are worked flat with a saddle shoulder.

✳ A circular needle is used to accommodate the large number of stitches.

Dec row: (WS) K2, ssk, work to last 4 sts, k2tog, k2—2 sts dec'd. Rep Dec Row every WS row 1 (3, 5, 5, 6) more time(s)—96 (112, 122, 130, 140) sts rem. Work even until armholes measure 7¾ (7¾, 8½, 8¾, 9¼)" (19.5 [19.5, 21.5, 22, 23.5] cm), ending with a WS row.

Right Cable

9 sts

Center Cable

24 sts

Left Cable

9 sts

☐ k on RS; p on WS	⧄	sl 2 sts onto cn, hold in back, k2, p2 from cn
⊡ p on RS; k on WS	⧄	sl 2 sts onto cn, hold in front, p2, k2 from cn
⧄ sl 1 st onto cn, hold in back, k2, p1 from cn	⧄	sl 2 sts onto cn, hold in back, k2, k2 from cn
⧄ sl 2 sts onto cn, hold in front, p1, k2 from cn	⧄	sl 2 sts onto cn, hold in front, k2, k2 from cn

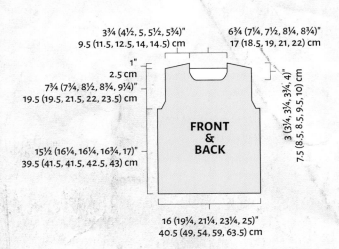

3¾ (4½, 5, 5½, 5¾)"
9.5 (11.5, 12.5, 14, 14.5) cm

6¾ (7¼, 7½, 8¼, 8¾)"
17 (18.5, 19, 21, 22) cm

1"
2.5 cm

7¾ (7¾, 8½, 8¾, 9¼)"
19.5 (19.5, 21.5, 22, 23.5) cm

3 (3¼, 3¼, 3¾, 4)"
7.5 (8.5, 8.5, 9.5, 10) cm

FRONT & BACK

15½ (16¼, 16¼, 16¾, 17)"
39.5 (41.5, 41.5, 42.5, 43) cm

16 (19¼, 21¼, 23¼, 25)"
40.5 (49, 54, 59, 63.5) cm

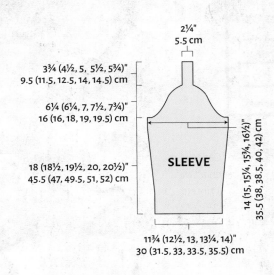

2¼"
5.5 cm

3¾ (4½, 5, 5½, 5¾)"
9.5 (11.5, 12.5, 14, 14.5) cm

6¼ (6¼, 7, 7½, 7¾)"
16 (16, 18, 19, 19.5) cm

14 (15, 15¾, 15¾, 16½)"
35.5 (38, 38.5, 40, 42) cm

18 (18½, 19½, 20, 20½)"
45.5 (47, 49.5, 51, 52) cm

SLEEVE

11¾ (12½, 13, 13¼, 14)"
30 (31.5, 33, 33.5, 35.5) cm

Shape Neck and Shoulders

Mark center 46 (50, 52, 56, 60) sts.

NEXT ROW: (RS) BO 8 (10, 11, 12, 13) sts, work to m, join new yarn and BO 46 (50, 52, 56, 60) sts for neck, work to end of row—17 (21, 24, 25, 27) sts rem for right back, 25 (31, 35, 37, 40) sts for left back. Working each side separately, BO 8 (10, 11, 12, 13) sts at beg of next row, then BO 8 (10, 12, 12, 13) sts at beg of foll 2 rows, then BO 9 (11, 12, 13, 14) sts at beg of foll 2 rows—no sts rem.

Front

Work as for back until armholes measure 5¾ (5½, 6¼, 6, 6¼)" (14.5 [14, 16, 15, 16] cm), ending with a WS row.

Shape Neck

NEXT ROW: (RS) Work 33 (40, 44, 47, 50) sts, join new yarn and BO 30 (32, 34, 36, 40) sts, work to end—33 (40, 44, 47, 50) sts rem each side. Working each side separately, dec 1 st at each neck edge every row 8 (9, 9, 10, 10) times—25 (31, 35, 37, 40) sts rem each side. Work even until armholes measure 7¾ (7¾, 8½, 8¾, 9¼)" (19.5 [19.5, 21.5, 22, 23.5] cm), ending with a WS row.

Shape Shoulders

BO 8 (10, 11, 12, 13) sts at beg of next 2 rows, then BO 8 (10, 12, 12, 13) sts at beg of foll 2 rows, then BO 9 (11, 12, 13, 14) sts at beg of foll 2 rows—no sts rem.

Sleeves

With smaller needle, CO 61 (65, 67, 69, 73) sts. Do not join. Work in k1, p1 rib until piece measures 1½" (3.8 cm) from CO, ending with a WS row. Change to larger needle.

NEXT ROW: (RS) P26 (28, 29, 30, 32), work Row 1 of Right Cable chart over 9 sts, p26 (28, 29, 30, 32). Work 13 (15, 15, 17, 17) rows even in patt, ending with a WS row. Inc 1 st each end of needle on next row, then every 14 (16, 16, 18, 18) rows 5 more times—73 (77, 79, 81, 85) sts. Work even in patt until piece measures 18 (18½, 19½, 20, 20½)" (45.5 [47, 49.5, 51, 52] cm) from CO, ending with a WS row.

Shape cap

BO 3 (4, 5, 6, 7) sts at beg of next 2 rows—67 (69, 69, 69, 71) sts rem. Dec 1 st each end of needle every row 4 (0, 0, 0, 0) times, then every RS row 15 (16, 19, 6, 8) times, then every 4th row 0 (0, 0, 4, 3) times, then every RS row 0 (0, 0, 6, 8) times—29 (37, 31, 37, 33) sts rem. BO 3 sts at beg of next 4 rows, then BO 2 (3, 3, 3, 4) sts at beg of foll 2 (4, 2, 4, 2) rows—13 sts rem.

Saddle

Work even until piece measures 3¾ (4½, 5, 5½, 5¾)" (9.5 [11.5, 12.5, 14, 14.5] cm) from last BO, or width of one shoulder. BO all sts.

Finishing

Block pieces to measurements. With yarn threaded on a tapestry needle, sew saddle to front and back shoulders. Sew sleeves into armholes. Sew sleeve and side seams.

Neckband

With 16" (40.5 cm) cir needle and RS facing, pick up and knit 126 (134, 140, 154, 162) sts around neck opening. Place marker (pm) and join in the rnd. Work in k1, p1 rib until piece

measures 1" (2.5 cm) from pick-up rnd. BO all sts in patt. Weave in loose ends. Block again, if desired. ✦

JOSIE MERCIER has been designing knitwear since 2005, and her designs include a pair of fantasy pointed ears, a pullover with pagan influences, and a line of patterns inspired by J. R. R. Tolkien's novel *The Hobbit*. Josie lives in Belleville, Ontario, Canada, and can be found online at mercierknittingpatterns.blogspot.com or on Ravelry as Pibble.

Fire to the south, Air to the east, Water to the west, Earth to the nor...

Lady of the House Wrapper

⁂ Vicki Square

*A*ncient family manors can be drafty, even when you have magic at your beck and call. This wrapper is what you need to keep the chill at bay. The tapered arms and snug fit mean that you won't be in danger of snagging your sleeves if, perchance, prisoners escape from your dungeon and a battle ensues.

Finished Size

14¾ (17, 18, 20¼, 22¼, 24½, 26¾)" (37.5 [43, 45.5, 51.5, 56.6, 62, 68] cm) back width. Wrapper shown measures 17" (43 cm).

Yarn

Madelintosh Tosh Sock (100% wool; 395 yd [361 m]/4¼ oz [120 g]): cosmos, 3 hanks for all sizes.

Needles

Size 3 (3.25 mm): 24" (61 cm) circular (cir). *Adjust needle size if necessary to obtain the correct gauge.*

Notions

Removable markers (m); waste yarn; stitch holder; tapestry needle; stickpin closure.

Gauge

22 sts and 38 rows = 4" (10 cm) in lace patt.

NOTE

*⁕ This lace wrapper is knitted in one piece begin-
ning at the lower edge of the back, casting on and
binding off for the sleeves. It is separated at the
back neck and each front is worked separately.
Keep continuity of lace pattern throughout.*

Back

CO 81 (93, 99, 111, 123, 135, 147) sts.

ROW 1: (RS) *P1, k1; rep from * to last st, p1.

ROW 2: (WS) *K1, p1; rep from * to last st, k1.

Work rows 1–6 of Lace chart, ending with a WS row.

Sleeves

Shape sleeves

Note: *Work new sts in lace patt and slip m when you come to them.*

NEXT ROW: (RS) Place marker (pm), using the cable method
(see Glossary), CO 3 sts, place marker (pm), work in patt to
end—3 sts inc'd for sleeve.

NEXT ROW: (WS) Pm, using the cable method, CO 3 sts, work in
patt to end—3 sts inc'd for sleeve.

NEXT ROW: (RS) Using the cable method, CO 3 sts, work in patt
to end—3 sts inc'd.

NEXT ROW: (WS) Using the cable method, CO 3 sts, work in
patt to end—3 sts inc'd. Rep last 2 rows 20 (20, 20, 21, 21, 21, 21)
more times, ending with a WS row—213 (225, 231, 249, 261, 273,
285) sts total: 66 (66, 66, 69, 69, 69, 69) sts for each sleeve; 81
(93, 99, 111, 123, 135, 147) sts for back.

NEXT ROW: (RS) Using the cable method, CO 6 sts, work in patt
to end—6 sts inc'd for sleeve.

NEXT ROW: (WS) Using the cable method, CO 6 sts, work in patt
to end—6 sts inc'd for sleeve. Rep last 2 rows 4 more times,
ending with a WS row—273 (285, 291, 309, 321, 333, 345) sts total;
96 (96, 96, 99, 99, 99, 99) sts for each sleeve before and after m,
81 (93, 99, 111, 123, 135, 147) sts for back. Work even in patt until

piece measures 9½ (9½, 10, 10, 10, 10½, 10½)" (24 [24, 25.5, 25.5,
25.5, 26.5, 26.5] cm) from CO edge, ending with a WS row.

Shape Back Neck

Work 123 (129, 132, 140, 146, 151, 157) sts in patt, BO 27 (27, 27, 29,
29, 31, 31) sts for center back, work in patt to end—123 (129, 132,
140, 146, 151, 157) sts rem each side. Place all sts for right sleeve
and shoulder on holder or waste yarn.

Left Front and Sleeve

Work 1 WS row even.

NEXT ROW: (RS) BO 6 sts pwise, work in patt to end—117
(123, 126, 134, 140, 145, 151) sts rem. Work 1 WS row in patt.
Place removable m into work at beg and end of row to mark
shoulder seam/halfway point and sleeve halfway point. Work
4 rows even in patt, ending with a WS row.

Shape Neck

INC ROW: (RS) K1, using the backward-loop method (see
Glossary), CO 1 st, work in patt to end—1 st inc'd at neck edge.
Rep Inc Row every other RS row 3 times, then every RS row 6
(6, 8, 8, 8, 10, 10) times—127 (133, 138, 146, 152, 159, 165) sts. Work
1 WS row in patt. Using the cable method, CO 2 sts at the beg
of next RS row, then CO 3 sts at the beg of the foll RS row, then
CO 5 sts at the beg of the foll RS row—137 (143, 148, 156, 162,
169, 175) sts. Work even in patt for 1" (2.5 cm) from last CO row,
ending with a WS row.

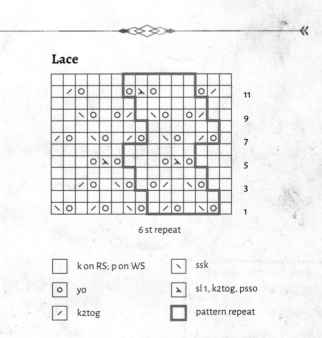

Lace

6 st repeat

☐ k on RS; p on WS   ＼ ssk

◯ yo   ⋏ sl 1, k2tog, psso

╱ k2tog   ☐ pattern repeat

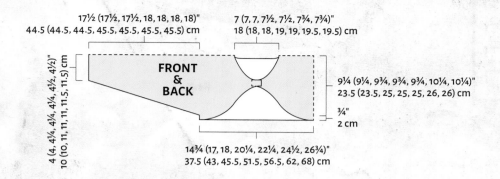

17½ (17½, 17½, 18, 18, 18, 18)"
44.5 (44.5, 44.5, 45.5, 45.5, 45.5, 45.5) cm

7 (7, 7, 7½, 7½, 7¾, 7¾)"
18 (18, 18, 19, 19, 19.5, 19.5) cm

FRONT & BACK

9¼ (9¼, 9¾, 9¾, 9¾, 10¼, 10¼)"
23.5 (23.5, 25, 25, 25, 26, 26) cm

¾"
2 cm

4 (4, 4¼, 4¼, 4¼, 4½, 4½)"
10 (10, 11, 11, 11, 11.5, 11.5) cm

14¾ (17, 18, 20¼, 22¼, 24½, 26¾)"
37.5 (43, 45.5, 51.5, 56.5, 62, 68) cm

Note: Front shaping and sleeve shaping happen at the same time. Read through the foll section before proceeding.

Shape Front

NEXT ROW: (RS) BO 4 (6, 6, 6, 7, 7, 7) sts, work in patt to end. Work 1 WS row in patt. BO 4 sts at the beg of next 0 (0, 0, 1, 1, 1, 2) RS row(s), then BO 3 sts at the beg of the foll 0 (1, 2, 1, 1, 2, 2) RS row(s), BO 2 sts at the beg of the foll 2 (1, 1, 1, 1, 0, 0) RS row(s)—8 (11, 14, 15, 16, 17, 21) sts dec'd at front edge. Work 1 WS row in patt.

DEC ROW: (RS) K1, k2tog, work in patt to end—1 st dec'd at front edge. Work 1 WS row in patt. Rep Dec Row every RS row 19 (19, 19, 19, 19, 21, 21) more times. Work 1 WS row in patt. BO 2 (3, 2, 3, 3, 3, 3) sts at beg of next RS row, then BO 4 (5, 3, 3, 4, 5, 5) sts at beg of next RS row, then BO 7 (8, 5, 6, 7, 8, 9) sts at beg of next RS row—0 (0, 8, 10, 13, 15, 16) sts rem. BO all rem sts. *At the same time*, when work measures 4 (4, 4¼, 4¼, 4¼, 4½, 4½)" (10 [10, 11, 11, 11, 11.5, 11.5] cm) from m at cuff,

Shape Sleeve

BO 6 sts at beg of next 5 WS rows, then BO 3 sts at beg of next 22 (22, 22, 23, 23, 23, 23) WS rows—96 (96, 96, 99, 99, 99, 99) sleeve sts dec'd. Work even at sleeve edge while cont to shape front edge.

Right Front and Sleeve

Return 123 (129, 132, 140, 146, 151, 157) right sleeve and shoulder sts to needle. With WS facing, join yarn at neck edge.

NEXT ROW: (WS) BO 6 sts pwise, work in patt to end—117 (123, 126, 134, 140, 145, 151) sts rem. Work 2 rows even in patt. Place removable m into work at beg and end of row to mark shoulder seam/halfway point and sleeve halfway point. Work 4 rows even in patt, ending with a WS row.

Shape Neck

INC ROW: (RS) Work in patt to last st, using the backward-loop method, CO 1 st, k1—1 st inc'd at neck edge. Rep Inc Row every other RS row 3 times, then every RS row 6 (6, 8, 8, 8, 10, 10) times—127 (133, 138, 146, 152, 159, 165) sts. Work 2 rows even in patt. Using the cable method, CO 2 sts at the beg of next WS row, then CO 3 sts at the beg of the foll WS row, then CO 5 sts at the beg of the foll WS row—137 (143, 148, 156, 162, 169, 175) sts. Work even in patt for 1" (2.5 cm) from last CO row, ending with a RS row.

Note: Front shaping and sleeve shaping happen at the same time. Read through the foll section before proceeding.

Shape Front

NEXT ROW: (WS) BO 4 (6, 6, 6, 7, 7, 7) sts, work in patt to end. Work 1 RS row in patt. BO 4 sts at the beg of next 0 (0, 0, 1, 1, 1, 2) WS row(s), then BO 3 sts at the beg of the foll 0 (1, 2, 1, 1, 2, 2) WS row(s), BO 2 sts at the beg of the foll 2 (1, 1, 1, 1, 0, 0) WS row(s)—8 (11, 14, 15, 16, 17, 21) sts dec'd at front edge.

DEC ROW: (RS) Work in patt to last 3 sts, ssk, k1—1 st dec'd at front edge. Work 1 WS row in patt. Rep Dec Row every RS row 19 (19, 19, 19, 19, 21, 21) more times. BO 2 (3, 2, 3, 3, 3, 3) sts at beg of next WS row, then BO 4 (5, 3, 3, 4, 5, 5) sts at beg of next WS row, then BO 7 (8, 5, 6, 7, 8, 9) sts at beg of next WS row—0 (0, 8, 10, 13, 15, 16) sts rem. BO all rem sts. At the same time, when work measures 4 (4, 4¼, 4¼, 4¼, 4½, 4½)" (10 [10, 11, 11, 11, 11.5, 11.5] cm) from m at cuff,

Shape Sleeve

BO 6 sts at beg of next 5 RS rows, then BO 3 sts at beg of next 22 (22, 22, 23, 23, 23, 23) RS rows—96 (96, 96, 99, 99, 99, 99) sleeve sts dec'd. Work even at sleeve edge while cont to shape front edge.

Finishing

Block and let dry completely.

Right Front Edging

Beg at right side seam, pick up and knit 60 (66, 68, 74, 80, 86, 92) sts evenly along curved lower edge of front to lower corner of center front, pick up and knit 7 sts along 1" (2.5 cm) of center front—67 (73, 75, 81, 87, 93, 99) sts, turn.

ROW 1: (WS) *P1, k1; rep from * to last st, p1.

ROW 2: (RS) *K1, p1; rep from * to last st, k1.

BO all sts in patt.

Left Front Edging

Beg at upper corner of center front, pick up and knit 7 sts along 1" (2.5 cm) of center front, pick up and knit 60 (66, 68, 74, 80, 86, 92) sts along curved lower edge of left front—67 (73, 75, 81, 87, 93, 99) sts.

ROW 1: (WS) *P1, k1; rep from * to last st, p1.

ROW 2: (RS) *K1, p1; rep from * to last st, k1.

BO all sts in patt.

Neck Edging

Beg at front edge of right front, pick up and knit 43 (43, 45, 45, 45, 48, 48) sts along right front neck edge to m, pick up and knit 42 (42, 42, 44, 44, 46, 46) sts along curved back neck to next m, pick up and knit 43 (43, 45, 45, 45, 48, 48) sts along left front neck edge—128 (128, 132, 134, 134, 142, 142) sts. Do not join. Knit 1 WS row.

ROW 1: (RS) Sl 1 pwise with yarn in back, knit to end.

ROW 2: (WS) Sl 1 pwise with yarn in front, purl to end.

Rep last 2 rows until collar measures 1¼" (3.2 cm) from garter ridge. BO all sts. (Collar will roll naturally, revealing the purl side.)

Sleeve Edging

Pick up and knit 49 (49, 51, 51, 51, 53, 53) sts along cuff edge. Do not join. Knit 2 rows.

ROW 1: (WS) *P1, k1; rep from * to last st, p1.

ROW 2: (RS) *K1, p1; rep from * to last st, k1.

BO all sts in patt.

Fold work with WS tog lengthwise at shoulder and sleeves. Sew side seams using mattress st with ½ st seam allowance. Sew cuff rib and garter ridge using mattress st with ½ st seam allowance. With RS tog, work slip-stitch crochet seam (see Glossary) for sleeve seams. Weave in ends and lightly steam seams. 🦉

VICKI SQUARE of Fort Collins, Colorado, learned to knit from her grandmother more than fifty years ago and has been designing her own garments ever since. She is the author of a number of knitting books from Interweave in addition to the best-selling book, *The Knitter's Companion* (Interweave, 1996).

Lady of the House Wrapper

Chameleon Sweater

⁂ Laura Lynch

This sweater has multiple quick-change identities: A close-fitting tunic in a bulky-weight yarn is covered in wide, soft cables that evoke rippling fluidity. A coordinating laceweight oversweater can be added or removed to change the look. Please note that the lace has a tendency to grow widthwise when stored flat but will return to its proper blocked measurements after being hung or worn for a few minutes. Blocking is key to both sweaters fitting properly.

Finished Sizes

Main sweater 27½ (30¼, 35¾, 38½, 44, 46¾, 52)" (70 [77, 90.5, 98, 112, 118.5, 132] cm) bust circumference. Lace oversweater 37¾ (42¼, 46¾, 53¾, 58¼, 62¾, 67½)" (96, 107.5, 118.5, 136.5, 148, 159.5, 171.5] cm) bust circumference. Main sweater shown in size 30¼". Lace oversweater shown in size 42¼" (107.5 cm).

Yarn

Main sweater—Brown Sheep Company Shepherd's Shades (100% wool; 131 yd [118 m]/3½ oz [100 g]): #SS281 eggplant (MC), 7 (8, 8, 9, 10, 11, 11) skeins.
Lace oversweater—Brown Sheep Company Legacy Lace (75% superwash wool, 25% nylon; 1,500 yd [1,372 m]/6 oz [170 g]): #Lace90 electric violet (CC), 1 skein.

Needles

Main sweater—size 10 (6 mm): 24" (61 cm) circular (cir) and double-pointed (dpn); Lace oversweater—size 6 (4 mm): 24" (61 cm) and 16" (40.5 cm) cir and dpn. *Adjust needle sizes if necessary to obtain the correct gauge.*

Notions

Markers (m); cable needle (cn); stitch holders; tapestry needle.

Gauge

17½ sts and 22½ rows = 4" (10 cm) in cable patt with MC on larger needles; 3 multiples and 22 rows = 4" (10 cm) in lace patt with CC on smaller needles, blocked.

Stitch Guide

Sk2p: Sl 1 kwise, k2tog, pass slipped st over—2 sts dec'd.

RT: Knit two together, leaving stitches worked on left needle. Knit into first stitch again, dropping both stitches worked from left needle.

LT: Knit into the second stitch on left needle, leaving stitch worked on left needle. Work into first stitch on left needle, dropping both stitches worked from left needle.

NOTES

❋ *Due to the density of the cable pattern, the body of the main sweater will pull in much more than the gauge swatch as you are working. This will block back out to the correct measurements.*

❋ *The body of the oversweater is worked in the round to the underarms, then the front and back are worked separately back and forth.*

❋ *The body and sleeves of the main sweater are worked in the round from the bottom to the yoke, then the pieces are joined for working the yoke.*

❋ *Charts are worked both in the round and back and forth in rows.*

□	k on RS; p on WS
o	yo
╱	k2tog
╲	ssk
⋏	sl 1, k2tog, psso
□	pattern repeat
⟋⟍	sl 3 sts onto cn, hold in back, k3, k3 from cn
⟍⟋	sl 3 sts onto cn, hold in front, k3, k3 from cn

Lace Oversweater
Body

With CC and smaller 24" (61 cm) cir needles, CO 198 (222, 246, 282, 306, 330, 354) sts. Place marker (pm) and join in the rnd. Knit 1 rnd. Purl 1 rnd. Knit 1 rnd.

NEXT RND: *K2, pm, work Row 1 of Lace chart over 96 (108, 120, 138, 150, 162, 174) sts, pm, k1; rep from * once more. Cont in patt as established through Rnd 12 of the 6 (6, 6, 6, 7, 7, 7)th rep of chart. **DIVIDE FOR FRONT AND BACK:** Place last 99 (111, 123, 141, 153, 165, 177) sts on holder for back.

Front

NEXT ROW: (RS) Work in patt as established to last st, k1f&b—100 (112, 124, 142, 154, 166, 178) sts.

NEXT ROW: (WS) K2, work in patt to last 2 sts, k2. Working first and last 2 sts in garter st (knit every row), cont in patt as established through Row 12 of the 9 (9, 9, 9, 10, 11, 11)th rep of chart from CO.

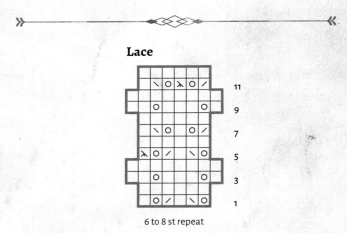

Lace

6 to 8 st repeat

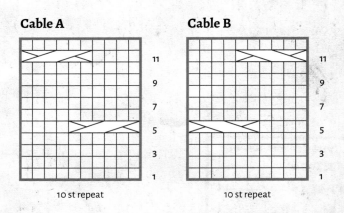

Cable A

10 st repeat

Cable B

10 st repeat

Shape Shoulders

Next 2 rows K20 (26, 32, 38, 44, 47, 53), work 60 (60, 60, 66, 66, 72, 72) in lace patt, k20 (26, 32, 38, 44, 47, 53). BO 20 (26, 32, 38, 44, 47, 53) at beg of next 2 rows—60 (60, 60, 66, 66, 72, 72) sts rem. Break yarn and place all sts on holder.

Back

Work as for front but do not break yarn.

Finishing

Neckband

Change to smaller 16" (40.5 cm) cir needle. Work in patt over 60 (60, 60, 66, 66, 72, 72) back neck sts, work in patt over 60 (60, 60, 66, 66, 72, 72) front neck sts from holder—120 (120, 120, 132, 132, 144, 144) sts total. Pm and join in the rnd. Cont in lace patt as established through Rnd 12 of the 12 (12, 12, 12, 13, 14, 14)th rep of chart from CO. Knit 1 rnd. Purl 1 rnd. Knit 1 rnd. BO all sts very loosely. Sew shoulder seams. Weave in ends. Block to measurements.

Main Sweater

Body

With MC and larger cir needles, CO 120 (132, 156, 168, 192, 204, 228) sts. Place marker (pm) and join in the rnd. Knit 1 rnd. Purl 1 rnd. Knit 1 rnd.

Sizes 27½ (38½)" only

SET-UP RND: P1, k1, p1, k2, [p2, work Cable A chart over 10 sts, p2, work Cable B chart over 10 sts] 2 (3) times, p2, k2, p1, k1, p1, pm, p1, k1, p1, k2, [p2, work Cable B chart over 10 sts, p2, work Cable A chart over 10 sts] 2 (3) times, p2, k2, p1, k1, p1.

Sizes 30¼ (52)" only

SET-UP RND: K2, [p2, work Cable A chart over 10 sts, p2, work Cable B chart over 10 sts] 2 (4) times, p2, work Cable A chart over 10 sts, p2, k2, pm, k2, [p2, work Cable B chart over 10 sts, p2, work Cable A chart over 10 sts] 2 (4) times, p2, work Cable B chart over 10 sts, p2, k2.

Sizes 35¾ (46¾)" only

SET-UP RND: K2, [p2, work Cable A chart over 10 sts, p2, work Cable B chart over 10 sts] 3 (4) times, p2, k2, pm, k2, [p2, work Cable B chart over 10 sts, p2, work Cable A chart over 10 sts] 3 (4) times, p2, k2.

Size 44" only

SET-UP RND: P1, k1, p1, k2, [p2, work Cable A chart over 10 sts, p2, work Cable B chart over 10 sts] 3 times, p2, work Cable A chart over 10 sts, p2, k2, p1, k1, p1, pm, p1, k1, p1, k2, [p2, work Cable B chart over 10 sts, p2, work Cable A chart over 10 sts] 3 times, p2, work Cable B chart over 10 sts, p2, k2, p1, k1, p1.

All Sizes

Work even in patt as established until piece measures 17 (18, 18, 18, 19, 19, 19)" (43 [45.5, 45.5, 45.5, 48.5, 48.5, 48.5] cm) from CO, ending with Row 12 of charts. Break yarn.

Sleeves

With MC and dpn, CO 36 sts. Pm and join in the rnd. Knit 1 rnd. Purl 1 rnd. Knit 1 rnd.

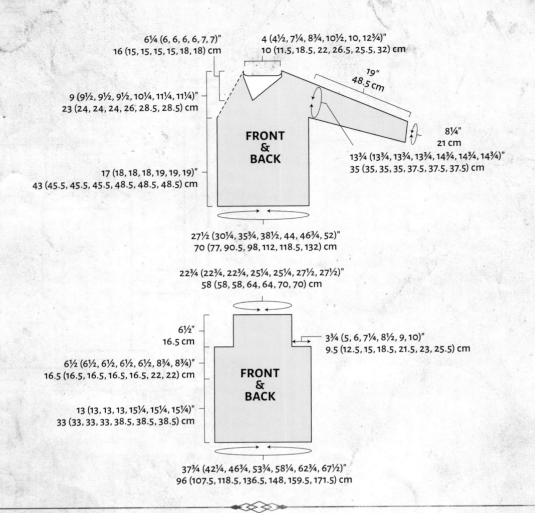

6¼ (6, 6, 6, 6, 7, 7)"
16 (15, 15, 15, 15, 18, 18) cm

4 (4½, 7¼, 8¾, 10½, 10, 12¾)"
10 (11.5, 18.5, 22, 26.5, 25.5, 32) cm

19"
48.5 cm

9 (9½, 9½, 9½, 10¼, 11¼, 11¼)"
23 (24, 24, 24, 26, 28.5, 28.5) cm

FRONT & BACK

8¼"
21 cm

13¾ (13¾, 13¾, 13¾, 14¾, 14¾, 14¾)"
35 (35, 35, 35, 37.5, 37.5, 37.5) cm

17 (18, 18, 18, 19, 19, 19)"
43 (45.5, 45.5, 45.5, 48.5, 48.5, 48.5) cm

27½ (30¼, 35¾, 38½, 44, 46¾, 52)"
70 (77, 90.5, 98, 112, 118.5, 132) cm

22¾ (22¾, 22¾, 25¼, 25¼, 27½, 27½)"
58 (58, 58, 64, 64, 70, 70) cm

6½"
16.5 cm

3¾ (5, 6, 7¼, 8½, 9, 10)"
9.5 (12.5, 15, 18.5, 21.5, 23, 25.5) cm

6½ (6½, 6½, 6½, 6½, 8¾, 8¾)"
16.5 (16.5, 16.5, 16.5, 16.5, 22, 22) cm

FRONT & BACK

13 (13, 13, 13, 15¼, 15¼, 15¼)"
33 (33, 33, 33, 38.5, 38.5, 38.5) cm

37¾ (42¼, 46¾, 53¾, 58¼, 62¾, 67½)"
96 (107.5, 118.5, 136.5, 148, 159.5, 171.5) cm

SET-UP RND: P1, work Cable A chart over 10 sts, p2, work Cable B chart over 10 sts, p2, work Cable A chart over 10 sts, p1. Work 11 rnds even in patt.

Note: *Work all new sts in p1, k1 rib.*

INC RND: M1L, work in patt to end, M1R—2 sts inc'd. Rep Inc Rnd every 6th rnd 7 (7, 7, 7, 9, 9, 9) times, then every 8th rnd 3 times, then every 10th rnd once—60 (60, 60, 60, 64, 64, 64) sts. Work even in patt until piece measures 19" from CO, ending with Row 12 of charts.

Yoke

JOINING RND: With larger cir needle, *K2 from sleeve, work rem sleeve sts in patt as established to last 2 sleeve sts rem, k2, pm, work 60 (66, 78, 84, 96, 102, 114) body sts to m, sl m, rep from * to end—240, (252, 276, 288, 320, 332, 356) sts.

Shape Armhole

RND 1: *K2, k2tog, work in patt to 4 sts before m, ssk, k2, sl m, rep from * 3 more times—8 sts dec'd.

RND 2: Work even in patt.

RND 3: *RT (see Stitch Guide), k2tog, work in patt to 4 sts before m, ssk, LT (see Stitch Guide), sl m, rep from * 3 more times—8 sts dec'd.

RND 4: Work even in patt.

Rep last 4 rnds 3 (4, 4, 4, 5, 5, 5) more times—176 (172, 196, 208, 224, 236, 260) sts rem.

Shape Neck

Note: *Beg working back and forth in rows. Raglan shaping is worked on the sleeves and back only.*

SET-UP ROW: (RS) *K2, k2tog, work in patt to 4 sts before m, ssk, k2, sl m, k2, work 28 (29, 37, 41, 53, 57, 58) sts in patt, place temporary m, sk2p (see Stitch Guide), ssk, work 7 (8, 12, 14, 17, 19, 23) sts in patt, k2, [sl m, k2, k2tog, work in patt to 4 sts before m, ssk, k2] 2 times—167 (163, 187, 199, 215, 227, 251) sts rem; 11 (12, 16, 18, 21, 23, 27) sts for right front, 30 (31, 39, 43, 48, 52, 60) sts for left front, 42 (44, 56, 62, 70, 76, 88) sts for back, 42 (38, 38, 38, 38, 38, 38) sts for each sleeve. Break yarn. With WS facing, rejoin yarn at temporary m and remove m.

ROWS 2, 4, 6, 8, 10: (WS) P1, p2tog, work in patt to last st, p1—1 st dec'd.

ROWS 3 AND 7: (RS) Work even in patt to 2 sts before 1st m, LT, *sl m, RT, k2tog, work in patt to 4 sts before next m, ssk, LT; rep from * 2 more times, sl m, RT, work even to last 3 sts, k2tog, k1—7 sts dec'd.

ROW 5: Work even in patt to 1st m, *sl m, k2, k2tog, work in patt to 4 sts before next m, ssk, k2; rep from * 2 more times, work even to last 3 sts, k2tog, k1—7 sts dec'd.

ROW 9: K1, sk2p, ssk, work to 1st m, *sl m, k2, k2tog, work in patt to 4 sts before next m, ssk, k2; rep from * 2 more times, work even to last 3 sts, k2tog, k1—10 sts dec'd.

Rep Rows 3–10 two (two, two, two, two, three, three) more times—61 (57, 81, 93, 109, 86, 110) sts rem; 2 (3, 7, 9, 12, 11, 15) sts for right front, 5 (6, 14, 18, 23, 19, 27) sts for left front, 18 (20, 32, 38, 46, 44, 56) sts for back, 18 (14, 14, 14, 14, 6, 6) sts for each sleeve.

NEXT ROW: (RS) Work even in patt to 2 sts before 1st m, LT, *sl m, RT, work in patt to 2 sts before next m, LT; rep from * two more times, sl m, RT, work in patt to last 3 sts, k2tog, k1—60 (56, 80, 92, 108, 85, 109) sts rem; 2 (3, 7, 9, 12, 11, 15) sts for right front, 4 (5, 13, 17, 22, 18, 26) sts for left front, 18 (20, 32, 38, 46, 44, 56) sts for back, 18 (14, 14, 14, 14, 6, 6) sts for each sleeve.

Shape Back Neck

NEXT ROW: (WS) P1, p2tog, work to 2 (3, 5, 5, 6, 6, 8) sts past 2nd m, join new ball of yarn and BO 14 (14, 22, 28, 34, 32, 40) center back sts, work even in patt to end—22 (20, 26, 28, 32, 23, 29) sts rem for right shoulder; 23 (21, 31, 35, 41, 29, 39) sts rem for left shoulder.

Shape Shoulders

NEXT ROW: (RS) Working both shoulders separately, on each shoulder, work even to m, sl m, k2, [k2tog] 3 (2, 2, 2, 2, 0, 0) times, [ssk] 4 (3, 3, 3, 3, 1, 1) times, k2, sl m, work in patt to end—15 (15, 21, 23, 27, 22, 28) sts rem for right shoulder; 16 (16, 26, 30, 36, 28, 38) sts rem for left shoulder. BO all rem sts.

Finishing

Neckband

With MC, dpn, and beg at back neck, pick up and knit 99 (105, 113, 121, 129, 139, 151) sts evenly around neck. Pm and join to work in the rnd. Purl 1 rnd. Knit 1 rnd. BO all sts pwise. Weave in ends. Block to measurements. 🐺

LAURA LYNCH was introduced to fantasy at a young age and began devouring all the stories about fairies, elves, wizards, and dragons she could find. She spends her time creating everything from pies to sweaters and incorporates her love of chocolate, bacon, and Star Wars (and other geeky things) into as many of her projects as possible. She does all this creating in northern New Jersey, and you can find her current blog at tastefuldiversions.wordpress.com.

Petal Socks

⚜ Rachel Coopey

These socks, inspired by spring blossoms that bring their own special kind of magic, feature twisted stitches and intricate petal motifs. The varigated yarn used here also hints at an inner darkness and complexity of character found in most spell-casters.

Finished Size

6¼ (7¼, 8¼)" (16 [18.5, 21] cm) foot circumference. Will stretch to fit foot circumference 8 (9, 10)" (20.5 [23, 25.5] cm) and leg length 6" (15 cm). Shown in size 7¼" (18.5 cm) foot circumference.

Yarn

Blue Moon Fiber Arts Socks That Rock Lightweight (100% superwash Merino; 405 yd [370 m]/5½ oz [155 g]): grawk, 1 skein.

Needles

Size 1½ (2.5 mm): set of double-pointed (dpn). *Adjust needle size if necessary to obtain the correct gauge.*

Notions

Stitch holder; tapestry needle.

Gauge

32 sts and 44 rnds = 4" (10 cm) in St st; 39 sts and 44 rnds = 4" (10 cm) in leg patt.

Socks

Cuff

CO 57 (66, 75) sts. Divide sts evenly over dpn and join in the rnd. Knit 7 rnds.

PICOT RND: *K2tog, yo; rep from * to last 1 (0, 1) st, k1 (0, 1). Knit 7 rnds. Fold cuff with WS tog at Picot Rnd.

JOINING RND: *Pick up 1 st from CO and place onto left needle, k2tog; rep from * around.

Leg

Work Rnds 1–6 of Leg chart for your size 10 times.

Heel Flap

Right sock only
K7 (9, 10).

Both socks
Heel is worked back and forth in rows over last 29 (34, 38) sts. Place rem 28 (32, 37) sts on holder for instep.

ROW 1: (WS) Sl 1 pwise with yarn in front (wyf), p28 (33, 37).

ROW 2: (RS) *Sl 1 pwise with yarn in back (wyb), k1; rep from * to last 1 (0, 0) st(s), k1 (0, 0).

Rep last 2 rows 15 more times, then work Row 1 once more.

Turn Heel

Work short-rows as foll:

SHORT-ROW 1: (RS) Sl 1 pwise wyb, k15 (18, 20), ssk, k1, turn.

SHORT-ROW 2: (WS) Sl 1 pwise wyf, p4 (5, 5), p2tog, p1, turn.

SHORT-ROW 3: (RS) Sl 1 pwise, wyb, knit to 1 st before gap, ssk, k1, turn.

SHORT-ROW 4: (WS) Sl 1 pwise wyf, purl to 1 st before gap, p2tog, p1, turn.

Rep last 2 short-rows 4 (5, 6) more times, ending with a WS row—17 (20, 22) heel sts rem.

Gusset

SET-UP RND: Sl 1 pwise wyb, k16 (19, 21), pick up and knit 16 sts along edge of heel flap (1 st in each chain-edge st), work Instep chart for your size over 28 (32, 37) instep sts, pick up and knit 16 sts along edge of heel flap, k33 (36, 38)—77 (84, 91) sts. Rnd beg at instep.

Note: Work through Rnd 12 of Instep chart once, then rep Rnds 7–12.

DEC RND: Work in patt over 28 (32, 37) instep sts, ssk, knit to last 2 sts, k2tog—2 sts dec'd.

NEXT RND: Work in patt over instep sts, knit to end.

Rep last 2 rnds 9 (9, 7) more times—57 (64, 75) sts rem.

Sizes 6¼" and 8¼" only
NEXT RND: Work in patt over instep sts, ssk, knit to end—56 (74) sts rem.

Right Instep size 6¼"

6-row rep

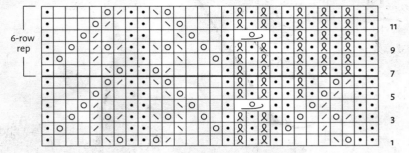

28 sts

11
9
7
5
3
1

Right Instep size 7¼"

6-row rep

32 sts

11
9
7
5
3
1

Right Instep size 8¼"

6-row rep

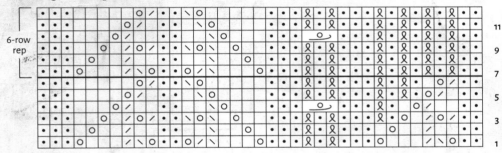

37 sts

11
9
7
5
3
1

□		knit
·		purl
o		yo
╱		k2tog
╲		ssk
ℛ		k1tbl
□		pattern repeat
‿o‿		pass 3rd st on left needle over first 2 sts, k1, yo, k1

All Sizes

Foot

Working in charted patt on instep sts and St st on sole sts, work even in patt until foot measures 2" (5 cm) less than desired finished length.

Toe

DEC RND: K1, ssk, knit to last 3 sts of instep, k2tog, k2, ssk, knit to last 3 sts of sole, k2tog, k1—4 sts dec'd.

NEXT RND: Knit.

Rep last 2 rnds 8 (10, 12) more times—20 (20, 22) sts rem. Break yarn, leaving a 12" (30.5 cm) tail.

Finishing

With tail threaded on a tapestry needle, graft sts using Kitchener st (see Glossary). Weave in ends and block.

RACHEL COOPEY of Worcestershire, United Kingdom, loves designing and knitting socks. You can read about her constant quest for warm feet, her ever-growing sock-yarn collection, and her knitting and spinning adventures on her blog, coopknits.co.uk, and find her on Ravelry as Coopknit.

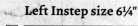

Left Instep size 6¼"

6-row rep

			11
			9
			7
			5
			3
			1

28 sts

Left Instep size 7¼"

6-row rep

32 sts

Left Instep size 8¼"

6-row rep

37 sts

Legend

- ☐ knit
- · purl
- ○ yo
- ╱ k2tog
- ╲ ssk
- ⅄ k1tbl
- ☐ pattern repeat
- 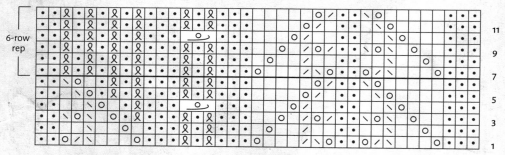 pass 3rd st on left needle over first 2 sts, k1, yo, k1

Leg size 6¼"

19 st repeat

Leg size 7¼"

22 st repeat

Leg size 8¼"

25 st repeat

Aviary Vest

⚜ Kyle Kunnecke

We are surrounded by superheroes. Firefighters, nannies, doctors, and teachers may quietly pass by us on the street, but when duty calls, they leap into action. The Aviary Vest is inspired by this idea of "hidden identity." Worn with a jacket, it's an unassuming, timeless vest. When the jacket is removed, the back reveals an intricately stranded wing pattern, symbolizing the wearer's strengths and abilities.

This project is worked flat and requires intermediate knitting knowledge, including stranded knitting, managing floats, simple shaping, and finishing. One row at a time, the knitter will gain confidence and learn that with ordinary determination and practice, something wonderful can happen.

Finished Size

38 (42, 45½, 50, 54)" (96.5 [106.5, 115.5, 127, 137] cm) chest circumference. Vest shown measures 45½" (115.5 cm).

Yarn

Zitron Lifestyle (100% extrafine superwash Merino; 170 yd [155 m]/1¾ oz [50 g]): #54 nutmeg (MC), 7 (8, 9, 10, 12) balls; #33 corn (CC), 2 balls. Yarn distributed by Skacel.

Needles

Body—size 3 (3.25 mm): 24" (61 cm) circular (cir). *Ribbing*—size 2 (2.75 mm): 16" (40.5 cm) and 24" (61 cm) cir. *Adjust needle size if necessary to obtain the correct gauge.*

Notions

Markers (m); stitch holders; tapestry needle.

Gauge

27 sts and 37 rows = 4" (10 cm) in St st on larger needle.

NOTES

✳ *The chart shows half of the wing pattern. Work each row of the chart to the end, then repeat the same row in reverse for the second half of the pattern.*

✳ *Work the chart using the stranded-knitting technique. Strand the unused yarn loosely across the back.*

✳ *To avoid long floats at the bottom and top of the chart, use separate balls of CC for each half of the chart through Row 110, then use 1 ball of CC through Row 174, then use two balls of CC to the end of the chart. At the end of each section of CC, twist MC and CC together as for intarsia knitting to avoid holes.*

Back

With MC and smaller needle, CO 128 (142, 154, 168, 182) sts. Do not join. Work in k2, p2 rib until piece measures 2½" (6.5 cm) from CO. Change to larger needle. Work in St st until piece measures 3½ (4¾, 5¼, 5½, 6½)" (9 [12, 13.5, 14, 16.5] cm) from CO, ending with a RS row.

NEXT ROW: (WS) P14 (21, 27, 34, 41), place marker (pm), p50, pm, p50, pm, purl to end.

NEXT ROW: Work in St st to m, work Row 1 of Wings chart to m, then, reading chart from left to right (see Notes), work Wings chart to m, work in St st to end. Cont in patt until piece measures 16 (16, 16, 16½, 17)" (40.5 [40.5, 40.5, 42, 43] cm) from CO, ending with a WS row.

Shape Armholes

Cont in patt, BO 4 (4, 4, 5, 6) sts at beg of next 2 rows, then BO 3 sts at beg of foll 2 rows—114 (128, 140, 152, 164) sts rem. BO 2 sts at beg of next 2 (4, 4, 4, 6) rows—110 (120, 132, 144, 152) sts rem.

DEC ROW: (RS) K2, k2tog, work in patt to last 4 sts, ssk, k2—2 sts dec'd. Rep Dec Row every RS row 1 (0, 4, 8, 11) more time(s)—106 (118, 122, 126, 128) sts rem. Work even in patt until armholes measure 7½ (8¾, 9¼, 9¼, 9½)" (19 [22, 23.5, 23.5, 24] cm), ending with a WS row.

Note: *After chart is complete, work all sts with MC.*

Shape Shoulders

Shape shoulders using short-rows (see Glossary) as foll:

SHORT-ROWS 1 AND 2: Work to last 7 (8, 9, 10, 11) sts, wrap next st, turn.

SHORT-ROWS 3 AND 4: Work to last 15 (17, 18, 18, 19) sts, wrap next st, turn.

SHORT-ROWS 5 AND 6: Work to last 22 (25, 26, 27, 28) sts, wrap next st, turn.

NEXT ROW: (RS) Work to end of row, working wraps tog with wrapped sts as you come to them.

NEXT ROW: (WS) Work to end of row, working rem wraps.

NEXT ROW: BO 29 (33, 34, 35, 36) sts, k48 (52, 54, 56, 56), BO 29 (33, 34, 35, 36) sts. Place 48 (52, 54, 56, 56) sts on holder for neck.

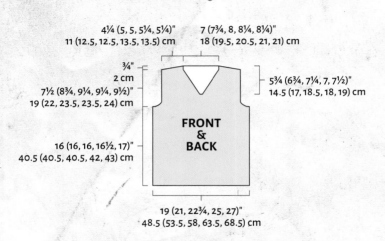

4¼ (5, 5, 5¼, 5¼)"
11 (12.5, 12.5, 13.5, 13.5) cm

7 (7¾, 8, 8¼, 8¼)"
18 (19.5, 20.5, 21, 21) cm

¾"
2 cm

7½ (8¾, 9¼, 9¼, 9½)"
19 (22, 23.5, 23.5, 24) cm

5¾ (6¾, 7¼, 7, 7½)"
14.5 (17, 18.5, 18, 19) cm

FRONT & BACK

16 (16, 16, 16½, 17)"
40.5 (40.5, 40.5, 42, 43) cm

19 (21, 22¾, 25, 27)"
48.5 (53.5, 58, 63.5, 68.5) cm

Front

With MC, work as for back, omitting chart and m, until armholes measure 2½ (2¾, 2¾, 3, 2¾)" (6.5 [7, 7, 7.5, 7] cm), ending with a WS row. **NOTE:** *Armhole shaping may not be complete; finish armhole shaping while working neck shaping.*

Shape Neck

Mark center 2 sts.

NEXT ROW: (RS) Work to m, place next 2 sts on holder for neck, place foll sts on holder for right front.

Left Front

Work 1 WS row.

DEC ROW: (RS) Knit to last 3 sts, k2tog, k1—1 st dec'd. Rep Dec Row every RS row 22 (24, 25, 26, 26) more times—29 (33, 34, 35, 36) sts rem. Work even until armhole measures 7½ (8¾, 9¼, 9¼, 9½)" (19 [22, 23.5, 23.5, 24] cm), ending with a RS row.

Shape Shoulder

Shape shoulder using short-rows as foll:

SHORT-ROW 1: (WS) Work to last 7 (8, 9, 10, 11) sts, wrap next st, turn, (RS) work to end.

SHORT-ROW 2: (WS) Work to last 15 (17, 18, 18, 19) sts, wrap next st, turn, (RS) work to end.

SHORT-ROW 3: (WS) Work to last 22 (25, 26, 27, 28) sts, wrap next st, turn, (RS) work to end.

NEXT ROW: (WS) Work to end, working wraps tog with wrapped sts as you come to them. BO all sts.

Right Front

Note: *Work armhole shaping at the same time as neck shaping if necessary. With RS facing, rejoin yarn to right front sts. Work 1 RS row, then 1 WS row.*

DEC ROW: (RS) K1, ssk, work to end—1 st dec'd. Rep Dec Row every RS row 22 (24, 25, 26, 26) more times—29 (33, 34, 35, 36) sts rem. Work even until armhole measures 7½ (8¾, 9¼, 9¼, 9½)" (19 [22, 23.5, 23.5, 24] cm), ending with a WS row.

Shape Shoulder

Shape shoulder using short-rows as foll:

SHORT-ROW 1: (RS) Work to last 7 (8, 9, 10, 11) sts, wrap next st, turn, (WS) work to end.

SHORT-ROW 2: (RS) Work to last 15 (17, 18, 18, 19) sts, wrap next st, turn, (WS) work to end.

SHORT-ROW 3: (RS) Work to last 22 (25, 26, 27, 28) sts, wrap next st, turn, (WS) work to end.

NEXT ROW: (RS) Work to end, working wraps tog with wrapped sts as you come to them. BO all sts.

Finishing

Block pieces to measurements. Sew shoulder and side seams.

Neckband

With RS facing, MC, and smaller 16" (40.5 cm) cir needle, beg at center front neck, k2 held sts, pick up and knit 54 (62, 66, 65, 68) sts along right neck to shoulder, k48 (52, 54, 56, 56) back neck sts from holder, pick up and knit 54 (62, 66, 65, 68) sts down left neck to base of V—158 (178, 188, 188, 194) sts total. Pm and join in the rnd.

NEXT RND: K2, k2tog, *p1, k1; rep from * to last 2 sts, ssk—156 (176, 186, 186, 192) sts rem.

DEC RND: K2, k2tog, work in rib to last 2 sts, ssk—2 sts dec'd. Rep Dec Rnd every rnd until piece measures 1" (2.5 cm) from pick-up rnd. BO all sts in patt.

Armhole Trim

With RS facing, MC, and smaller 16" (40.5 cm) cir needle, beg at side seam, pick up and knit 114 (132, 140, 140, 144) sts evenly spaced around armhole opening. Pm and join in the rnd. Work in k1, p1 rib until piece measures 1" (2.5 cm) from pick-up rnd. BO all sts in patt. Weave in loose ends. Block again, if needed. 🦅

AT KYLE Kunnecke's San Francisco studio, he does his best to translate experiences into work that inspires awareness, involvement, and action. He believes creativity has the power to heal, and that we all have the ability to make a difference in our communities. Visit his website to learn more, kylewilliam.com.

Wings (lower half)

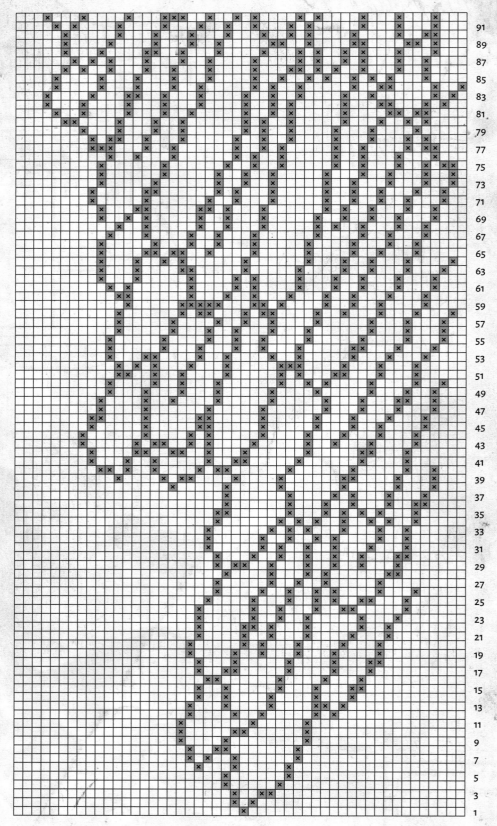

91
89
87
85
83
81
79
77
75
73
71
69
67
65
63
61
59
57
55
53
51
49
47
45
43
41
39
37
35
33
31
29
27
25
23
21
19
17
15
13
11
9
7
5
3
1

50 sts

185
183
181
179
177
175
173
171
169
167
165
163
161
159
157
155
153
151
149
147
145
143
141
139
137
135
133
131
129
127
125
123
121
119
117
115
113
111
109
107
105
103
101
99
97
95
93

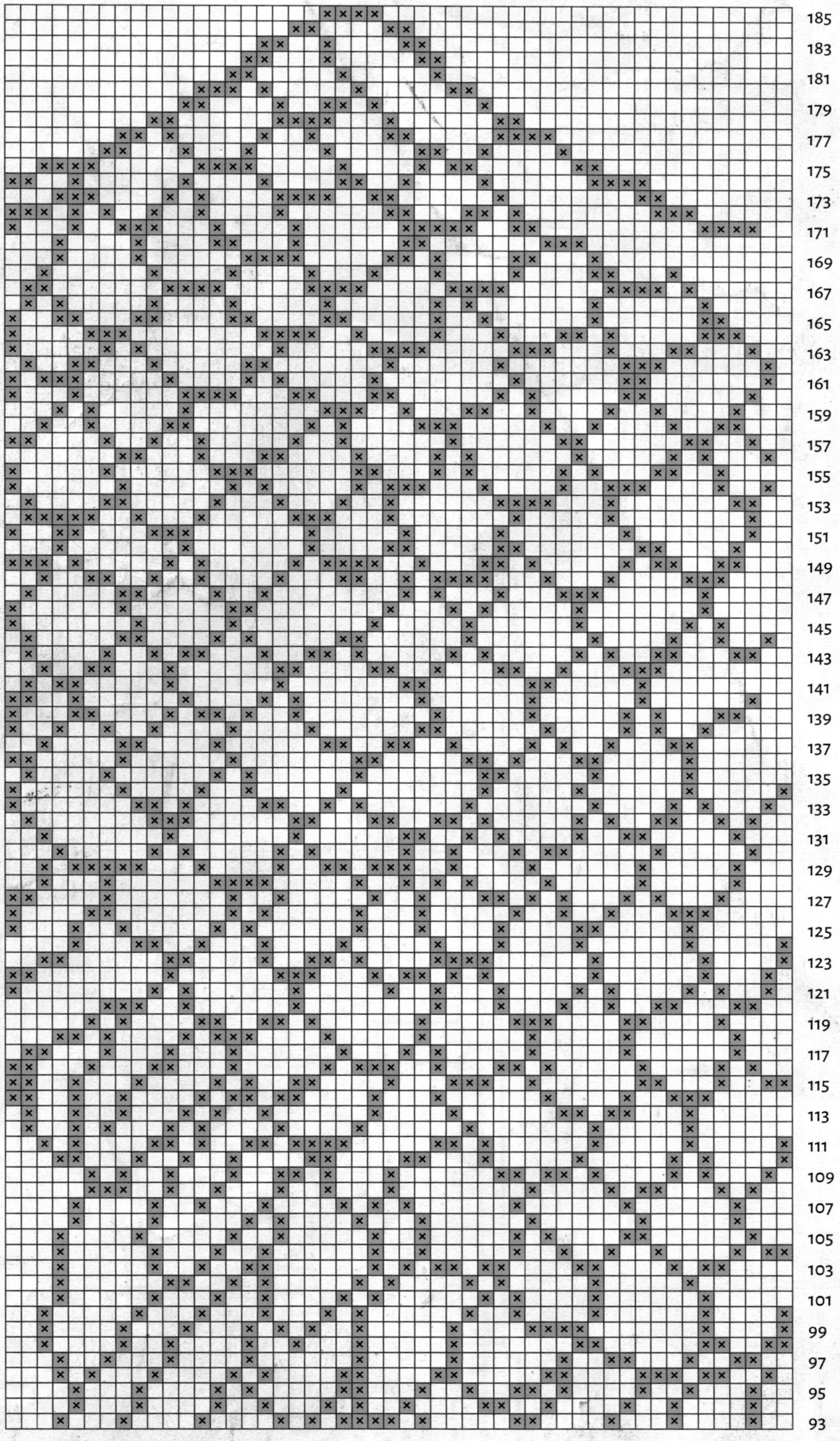

Lacy Cloak

⚜ Catherine Salter Bayar

*D*abbling in the Dark Arts means that you will undoubtedly encounter those who have more than a smidge of untempered lunacy about them—not unlike this intricate maze of lace. A large collar wraps the neck and front and rounds the bottom to become the hem, creating an airy cocoon of interlocking pattern, suitable for witches who love to knit. Typically, cloaks have no sleeves, yet adding them is more practical for modern witchery.

Finished Size
30 (36, 42)" (76 [91.5, 106.5] cm) bust circumference. Cloak shown measures 30" (76 cm).

Yarn
Hand Maiden Mini Maiden (50% wool, 50% silk; 547 yd [500 m]/3½ oz [100 g]): ebony, 5 (6, 7) skeins.

Yarn distributed by ColorSong Yarn.

Needles
Sizes 1½ (2.5 mm) and 3 (3.25 mm): 24"–32" (61–81.5 cm) circular (cir). *Adjust needle size if necessary to obtain the correct gauge.*

Notions
Markers (m); stitch holder; waste yarn for easing sleeve cap; tapestry needle.

Gauge
28 sts and 34 rows = 4" (10 cm) in St st on larger needle; 1 body patt rep = 3" (7.5 cm) wide on larger needle.

NOTES

✳ *The body is worked in one piece from bottom to underarms, then divided into two fronts and a back and worked to the shoulders. The sleeves are worked separately and sewn in.*

✳ *The collar is worked around the fronts and neck, first on the right side, then on the wrong side, to create a pattern that folds at the rib section to the right side.*

✳ *The bottom edging is worked next and joined to the collar at the front corners to create the cloak's curved shape.*

✳ *A circular needle is used to accommodate the large number of stitches.*

Body

With larger needle, CO 215 (238, 261) sts. Do not join.

NEXT ROW: (RS) Work Edging chart over 4 sts, work Body chart to last 4 sts, work Edging chart over 4 sts. Cont in patt through Row 42 of Body chart, then work Rows 3–42 of chart 3 more times—251 (278, 305) sts.

Right Front

NEXT ROW: (RS) Work 58 sts in patt (to end of 2nd patt rep), place next 193 (220, 247) sts on holder—54 sts rem for right front. Cont in patt through Row 42 of chart, then work Rows 3–22 (3–22, 3–32) once more. BO all sts.

Back

With RS facing, rejoin yarn. Work 135 (162, 189) sts according to Row 3 of chart, leave next 58 sts on holder for left front—125 (150, 175) sts rem for back. Cont in patt through Row 42 of chart, then work Rows 3–22 (3–22, 3–32) once more. BO all sts.

Left Front

With RS facing, rejoin yarn to 58 held sts. Work Rows 3–42 of chart once, then work Rows 3–22 (3–22, 3–32) once more. BO all sts.

Edging

Body

Lower Edging

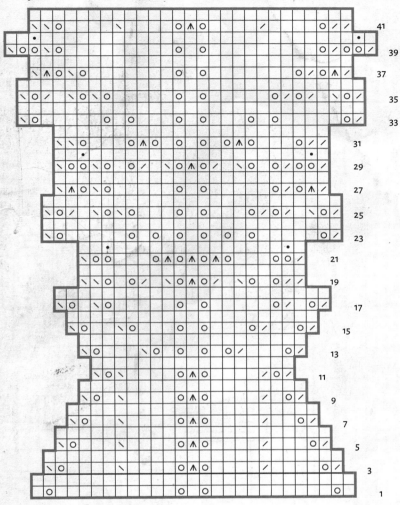

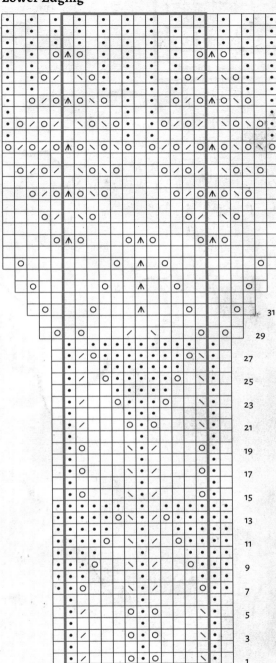

12 st repeat

☐ k on RS; p on WS

• p on RS; k on WS

◯ yo

╱ k2tog

╲ ssk

⅄ sl 2 as if to k2tog, k1, p2sso

▨ no stitch

☐ pattern repeat

Lacy Cloak ⬡141

Sleeve

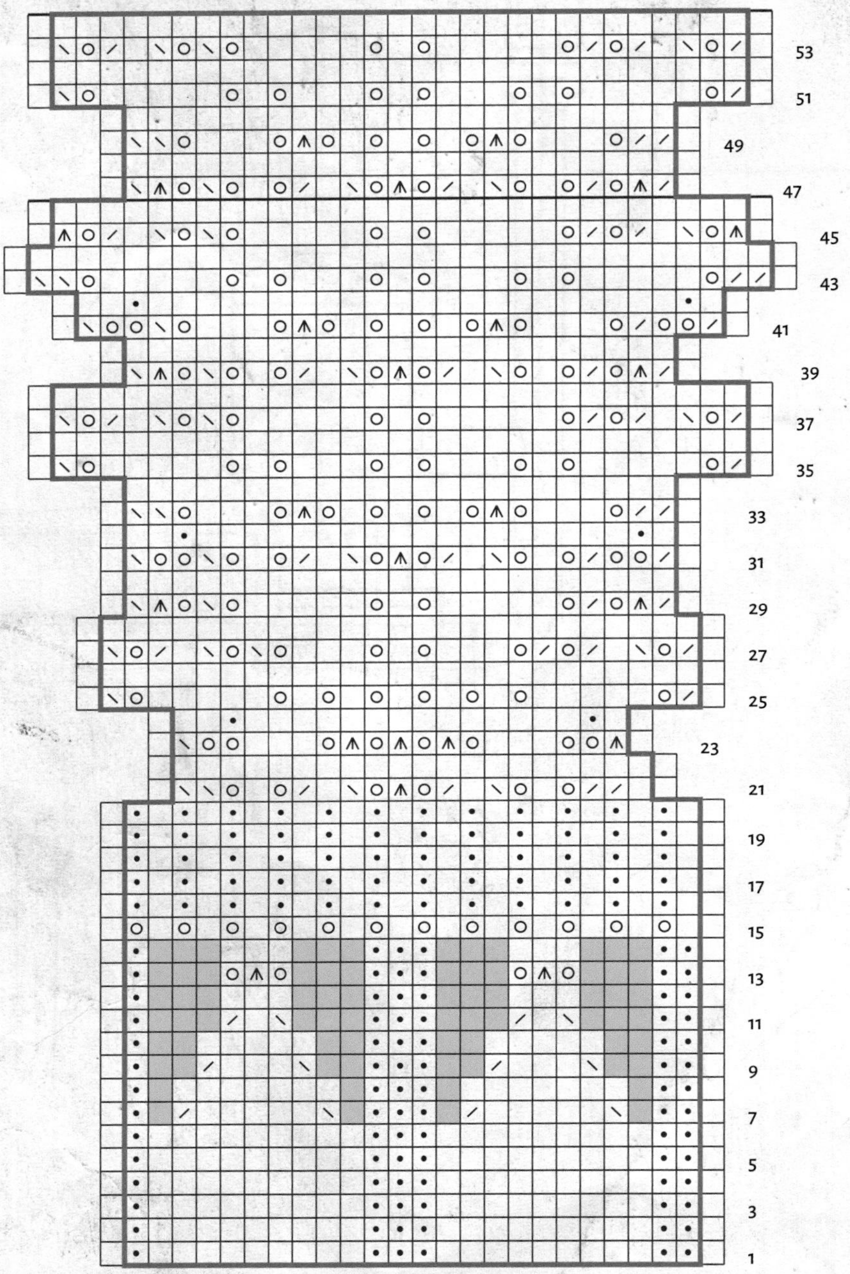

53
51
49
47
45
43
41
39
37
35
33
31
29
27
25
23
21
19
17
15
13
11
9
7
5
3
1

Collar

21
19
17
15
13
11
9
7
5
3
1

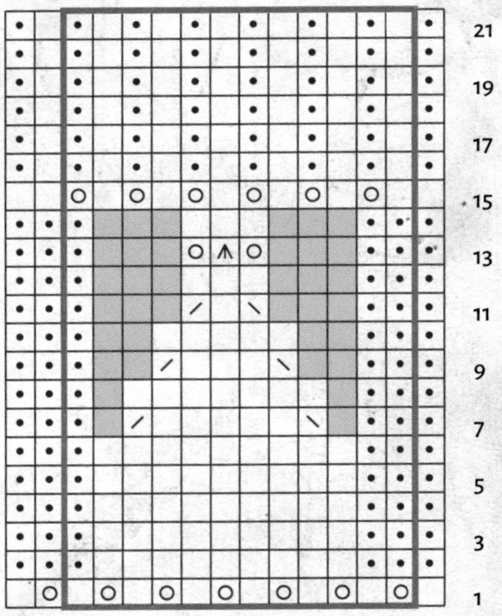

	k on RS; p on WS
•	p on RS; k on WS
O	yo
/	k2tog
\	ssk
⋀	sl 2 as if to k2tog, k1, p2sso
▨	no stitch
⬜	pattern repeat

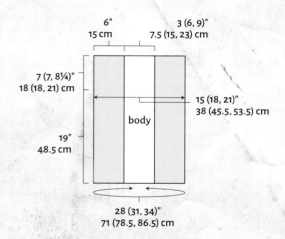

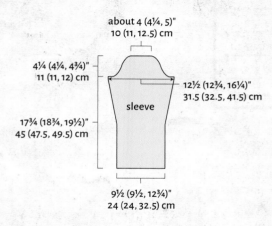

Sleeves

With smaller needle, CO 74 (74, 98) sts. Do not join. Work Rows 1–54 of Sleeve chart once, then rep Rows 47–54 four more times—89 (89, 118) sts. Change to larger needle. Work Rows 47–54 once more. Inc 1 st each end of needle on next row, then every 8th row 8 (9, 10) more times, working new sts into patt—89 (91, 116) sts. Work 1 WS row (Row 48 of chart).

Shape Cap

Cont in patt, BO 5 sts at beg of next 2 rows, then BO 3 sts at beg of foll 2 rows, then BO 2 sts at beg of foll 12 rows—Row 48 of chart is complete. Work Rows 49–54 once, then work Rows 47–54 once, then work Rows 47 and 48 once. BO 5 sts at beg of next 4 (4, 8) rows—Row 52 (52, 48) of chart is complete. Loosely BO all sts.

Finishing

Sew shoulder seams.

Collar

With smaller needle, RS facing, and beg at right front lower edge, pick up (but do not knit) 115 (115, 121) sts along right front to shoulder, 24 (48, 72) sts across back neck, and 115 (115, 121) sts down left front to lower edge—254 (278, 314) sts total. With RS facing and beg at right front lower edge, work Rows 1–21 of Collar chart once—507 (555, 627) sts.

Note: *At this point, WS of body becomes RS of collar; collar will fold back.*

With WS of body (new RS of collar) facing, work Rows 1–56 of Lower Edging chart once—515 (563, 635) sts. Loosely BO all sts in patt.

Lower Edging

With smaller needle, RS facing, and beg at Row 15 of Collar chart on left front, pick up (but do not knit) 243 (267, 291) sts along lower edge, ending at Row 15 of Collar chart on right front. With RS facing and beg at left front lower edge, work 6 rows in k1, p1 rib. Work Rows 1–56 of Lower Edging chart once and, *at the same time,* inc 1 st each end of needle every WS row, working new sts into patt. Loosely BO all sts in patt. Sew selvedge edge of collar to selvedge edge of lower edging. Sew sleeve seams. Run waste yarn through top of sleeve cap to ease cap evenly into armhole. Sew in sleeves. Remove waste yarn. Weave in loose ends. Very lightly block garment and collar points without losing texture of lace patt. 🦅

California native **CATHERINE SALTER BAYAR** is a clothing, interior, and knitwear designer who relocated to Turkey in 1999 to pursue her love of handmade textiles and fiber arts. Bazaar Bayar is a handcrafts workshop she founded in Istanbul to provide work for local artisans and to teach visiting women about Turkish handcrafts—both traditional and modern. Learn more at bazaarbayar.com.

Abbreviations

beg beginning; begin; begins

bet between

BO bind off

CC contrasting color

ch chain

cm centimeter(s)

cn cable needle

CO cast on

cont continue(s); continuing

dc double crochet

dec(s) decrease(s); decreasing

dpn double-pointed needle(s)

foll following; follows

g gram(s)

inc increase(s); increasing

k knit

k1f&b knit into front and back of same st

k2tog knit two stitches together

k3tog knit three stitches together

kwise knitwise

m(s) marker(s)

MC main color

mm millimeter(s)

M1 make one (increase)

p purl

p1f&b purl into front and back of same st

p2tog purl two stitches together

patt(s) pattern(s)

pm place marker

psso pass slipped stitch over

p2sso pass two slipped stitches over

pwise purlwise

rem remain(s); remaining

rep repeat; repeating

rev St st reverse stockinette stitch (purl on RS, knit on WS)

rib ribbing

rnd(s) round(s)

RS right side

sc single crochet

sk skip

sk2p slip 1 st kwise, k2tog, pass sl st over—2 sts dec'd

sl slip

sl st slip stitch (sl 1 st pwise unless otherwise indicated)

sp space

ssk slip 1 kwise, slip 1 kwise, k2 sl sts tog tbl (decrease)

sssk slip 3 sts kwise individually, then knit them tog tbl—2 sts dec'd

ssp slip 1 kwise, slip 1 kwise, p2 sl sts tog tbl (decrease)

st(s) stitch(es)

St st stockinette stitch (knit on RS, purl on WS)

tbl through back loop

tog together

WS wrong side

wyb with yarn in back

wyf with yarn in front

yo yarn over

* repeat starting point (i.e., repeat from *)

** repeat all instructions between asterisks

() alternate measurements and/or instructions

[] instructions that are to be worked as a group a specified number of times

Glossary

This book contains many patterns for intermediate to advanced knitters. A few patterns will appeal to beginning knitters as well. For those who are compelled to knit for the first time because of this publication, you'll find resources at your fingertips at *knittingdaily.com*.

2 (3, 4, 5) Stitch One-Row Buttonhole

Work to where you want the buttonhole to begin, bring yarn to front, slip one purlwise, bring yarn to back (*Figure 1*). *Slip one purlwise, pass first slipped stitch over second; repeat from * one (two, three, four) more time(s). Place last stitch back on left needle (*Figure 2*), turn. Cast on three (four, five, six) stitches as follows: *Insert right needle between the first and second stitches on left needle, draw up a loop, and place it on the left needle (*Figure 3*); repeat from * two (three, four, five) more times, turn. Bring yarn to back, slip first stitch of left needle onto right needle and pass last cast-on stitch over it (*Figure 4*), work to end of row.

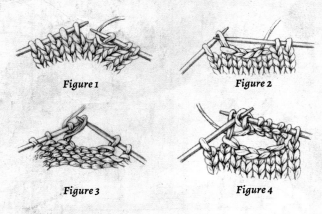

Figure 1   *Figure 2*

Figure 3   *Figure 4*

Cast-Ons

Backward-Loop Cast-On

*Loop working yarn and place it on needle backward so that it doesn't unwind. Repeat from *.

Cable Cast-On

Begin with a slipknot and one knitted cast-on stitch if there are no established stitches. Insert right needle between first two stitches on left needle (*Figure 1*). Wrap yarn as if to knit. Draw yarn through to complete stitch (*Figure 2*) and slip this new stitch to left needle as shown (*Figure 3*).

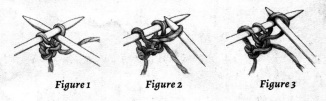

Figure 1   *Figure 2*   *Figure 3*

Continental (Long-Tail) Cast-On

Leaving a long tail (about ½" to 1" (2.5 cm) for each stitch to be cast on), make a slipknot and place on right needle. Place thumb and index finger of left hand between yarn ends so that working yarn is around index finger and tail end is around thumb. Secure ends with your other fingers and hold palm upward, making a V of yarn (*Figure 1*). Bring needle up through loop on thumb (*Figure 2*), grab first strand around index finger with needle, and go back down through loop on thumb (*Figure 3*). Drop loop off thumb and, placing thumb back in V configuration, tighten resulting stitch on needle (*Figure 4*).

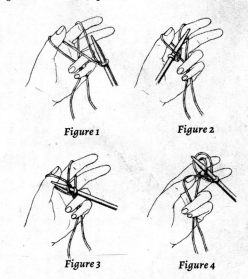

Figure 1   *Figure 2*

Figure 3   *Figure 4*

Judy's Magic Cast-On

Note: *Judy's magic CO was invented by Judy Becker as a CO for toe-up socks. The technique made its debut in the Spring 2006 issue of Knitty magazine, and her detailed tutorial can be found at www.knitty.com. The technique is modified here so that it uses a half-twist rather than a slipknot.*

Step 1: Hold one needle tip horizontally and drape the yarn over it with the tail toward you and the yarn going to the ball (working yarn) away from you. Give the yarn a half twist below the needle so that the tail is now away from you and the working yarn is toward you (the reverse of long-tail CO).

Step 2: Hold another needle tip just below the needle with the yarn loop already on it. The yarn loop will be the first st CO to the top needle. Tent the yarn strands over the thumb and index finger of your left hand as if doing a long-tail CO. The tail will rest on your index finger, and the working yarn will rest on your thumb.

Step 3: Cast the first st onto the bottom needle by bringing both needles up and around the yarn tail on your index finger, scooping up the yarn using a clockwise motion with your right hand. The yarn will wrap around the bottom of the empty bottom needle from back to front as for a yarnover. Sl the yarn tail between the needles to complete the loop around the bottom needle. There is now one st CO to each needle. Be sure to pull these first sts tight to avoid loose sts at the edge of the CO row.

Step 4: Cast the next st onto the top needle by bringing both needles down and around the working yarn on your thumb, scooping up the yarn using a counterclockwise motion with your right hand. The yarn will wrap around the top of the top needle from back to front. Sl the working yarn between the needles to complete the loop around the top needle.

Step 5: Cast the next st onto the bottom needle as in Step 3. Rep Steps 4–5 until there are the desired number of sts on each needle. Rotate needles so that the yarn tail and working yarn are on your right. The working yarn should be coming off the bottom needle and the yarn tail off the top needle. You will begin working across the sts on the top needle. Make sure to capture the yarn tail by placing it between the top needle and the working yarn as you start knitting across the sts on the top needle. You can pull the yarn tail to firm up any looseness at the beginning of this rnd.

Note: *When working the sts on the second (bottom) needle, you will need to knit them through the back loops to avoid twisting them.*

Knitted Cast-On

Place slipknot on left needle if there are no established stitches. *With right needle, knit into first stitch (or slipknot) on left needle **(Figure 1)** and place new stitch onto left needle **(Figure 2)**. Repeat from *, always knitting into last stitch made.

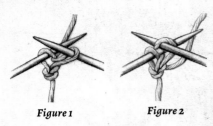

Figure 1   **Figure 2**

Old Norwegian Cast-On

Leaving a long tail, make a slipknot, and hold yarn as shown **(Figure 1)**. *Bring needle in front of thumb, under both yarns around thumb, down into center of thumb loop, back forward, and over top of yarn around index finger **(Figure 2)**, catch this yarn, and bring needle back down through thumb loop **(Figure 3)**, turning thumb slightly to make room for needle to pass through. Drop loop off thumb and place thumb back in V configuration while tightening up resulting stitch on needle **(Figure 4)**. Repeat from *.

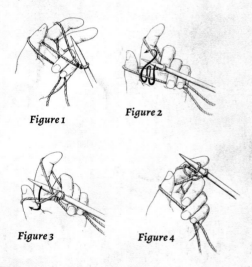

Figure 1   **Figure 2**

Figure 3   **Figure 4**

Provisional Cast-On

Place a loose slipknot on needle held in your right hand. Hold waste yarn next to slipknot and around left thumb; hold working yarn over left index finger. *Bring needle forward under waste yarn, over working yarn, grab a loop of working yarn (**Figure 1**), then bring needle to the front, over both yarns, and grab a second loop (**Figure 2**). Repeat from *. When you're ready to work in the opposite direction, pick out waste yarn to expose live stitches.

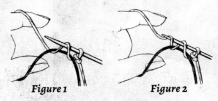

Figure 1   **Figure 2**

Crochet

Crochet Chain (ch)

Make a slipknot on hook. Yarn over hook and draw it through loop of slipknot. Repeat, drawing yarn through the last loop formed.

Slip-Stitch Crochet (sl st)

Insert hook into stitch, yarn over hook and draw loop through stitch and loop on hook.

Bind-Offs

I-Cord Bind-Off

When there are live stitches or picked-up stitches: With right side facing, cast on number of stitches directed in pattern onto left needle. *Knit to last I-cord stitch (e.g., if working a three-stitch I-cord, knit two), knit two together through the back loop, transfer all stitches from right needle to left needle; repeat from * for I-cord.

Sewn Bind-Off

Cut the yarn three times the width of the knitting to be bound off and thread onto a tapestry needle. Working from right to left, *insert tapestry needle purlwise (from right to left) through first two stitches (**Figure 1**) and pull the yarn through, then bring needle knitwise (from left to right) through the first stitch (**Figure 2**), pull the yarn through, and slip this stitch off the knitting needle. Repeat from *.

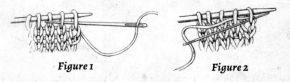

Figure 1   **Figure 2**

Three-Needle Bind-Off

Place stitches to be joined onto two separate needles. Hold them with right sides of knitting facing together. Insert a third needle into first stitch on each of the other two needles and knit them together as one stitch. *Knit next stitch on each needle the same way. Pass first stitch over second stitch. Repeat from * until one stitch remains on third needle. Cut yarn and pull tail through last stitch.

Increases

Lifted Increase

Knit into the back of stitch (in the "purl bump") in the row directly below the stitch on the left needle.

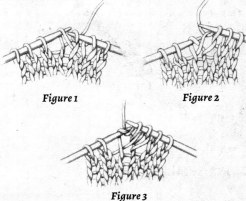

Figure 1   **Figure 2**

Figure 3

Make One Increases

Make one right (M1R): Insert left needle from back to front under strand of yarn running between last stitch on left needle and first stitch on right needle, then knit the lifted strand through its front loop—one stitch increased.

Make one left (M1L): Insert left needle from front to back under strand of yarn running between last stitch on left needle and first stitch on right needle, then knit the lifted strand through its back loop—one stitch increased.

Make one purl (M1P): Insert left needle from back to front under strand of yarn running between last stitch on left needle and first stitch on right needle, then purl the lifted strand through its front loop—one stitch increased.

Intarsia

Joining a New Color

Knit side: (RS) When the chart shows that the next stitch or set of stitches is worked in a new color, drop the old color to the WS of the work. *Insert the right needle into the next stitch as if to knit. Leaving a 4" (10 cm) tail of the new color, work the stitch with the new color. Let go of the new color, then pick up the strand of the old color and place it *over* the strand of the new color just worked. Keeping a slight tension on the old yarn, pick up the new yarn from *under* the old and make the next stitch with the new yarn *(Figure 1)*. Drop the old yarn and continue to work the stitches indicated on the chart for the new color. When it's time to change colors again, repeat from *. If the chart indicates that the next set of stitches is worked in a color that you've already used, start a brand-new strand of yarn or bobbin of that color. Don't carry the old strand across the back of the work.

Figure 1   **Figure 2**

Purl side: (WS) When the chart shows that the next stitch or set of stitches is worked in a new color, drop the old color to the WS (the side facing you). *Insert the right needle into the next stitch as if to purl. Leaving a 4" (10 cm) tail of the new color, work the stitch with the new color. Drop the new color. Pick up the strand of the old color and place it *over* the strand of the new color just worked. Keeping a slight tension on the old yarn, pick up the new yarn from *under* the old and make the next stitch with the new yarn *(Figure 2)*. Continue to work the stitches indicated on the chart for the new color. When it's time to change colors again, repeat from *.

Embellishments

Braid (Three Strand)

1. Begin with three strands or three groups of strands. Tie an overhand knot at one end *(Figure 1)*.

2. Lay the right strand over the middle strand. The right strand becomes the new middle strand.

3. Lay the left strand over the new middle strand *(Figure 2)*.

4. Repeat Steps 2 *(Figure 3)* and 3 *(Figure 4)* to desired length.

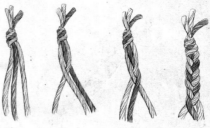

Figure 1   **Figure 2**   **Figure 3**   **Figure 4**

Duplicate Stitch

Horizontal: Bring threaded needle out from back to front at the base of the V of the knitted stitch you want to cover. *Working right to left, pass needle in and out under the stitch in the row above it and back into the base of the same stitch. Bring needle back out at the base of the V of the next stitch to the left. Repeat from *.

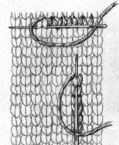

Vertical: Beginning at lowest point, work as for horizontal duplicate stitch, ending by bringing the needle back out at the base of the stitch directly above the stitch just worked.

I-Cord

With double-pointed needle, cast on desired number of stitches. *Without turning the needle, slide the stitches to other end of the needle, pull the yarn around the back, and knit the stitches as usual; repeat from * for desired length.

Pom-Pom

Cut two circles of cardboard, each ½" (1.3 cm) larger than desired finished pom-pom width. Cut a small circle out of the center and a small edge out of the side of each circle **(Figure 1)**. Tie a strand of yarn between the circles, hold circles together and wrap with yarn—the more wraps, the thicker the pom-pom. Cut between the circles and knot the tie strand tightly **(Figure 2)**. Place pom-pom between two smaller cardboard circles held together with a needle and trim the edges **(Figure 3)**. This technique comes from *Nicky Epstein's Knitted Embellishments* (Interweave, 1999).

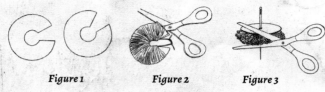

Figure 1   *Figure 2*   *Figure 3*

Grafting

Kitchener Stitch

Step 1: Bring threaded needle through front stitch as if to purl and leave stitch on needle.

Step 2: Bring threaded needle through back stitch as if to knit and leave stitch on needle.

Step 3: Bring threaded needle through first front stitch as if to knit and slip this stitch off needle. Bring threaded needle through next front stitch as if to purl and leave stitch on needle.

Step 4: Bring threaded needle through first back stitch as if to purl (as illustrated), slip this stitch off, bring needle through next back stitch as if to knit, leave this stitch on needle.

Repeat Steps 3 and 4 until no stitches remain on needles.

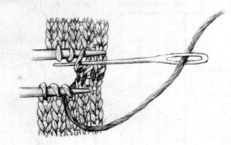

Short-Rows

Knit Side

Work to turning point, slip next stitch purlwise **(Figure 1)**, bring the yarn to the front, then slip the same stitch back to the left needle **(Figure 2)**, turn the work around and bring the yarn in position for the next stitch—one stitch has been wrapped and the yarn is correctly positioned to work the next stitch. When you come to a wrapped stitch on a subsequent knit row, hide the wrap by working it together with the wrapped stitch as follows: Insert right needle tip under the wrap from the front; **(Figure 3)**, then into the stitch on the needle, and work the stitch and its wrap together as a single stitch.

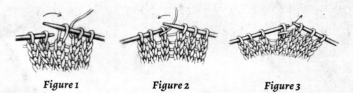

Figure 1   *Figure 2*   *Figure 3*

Purl Side

Work to the turning point, slip the next stitch purlwise to the right needle, bring the yarn to the back of the work **(Figure 1)**, return the slipped stitch to the left needle, bring the yarn to the front between the needles (Figure 2), and turn the work so that the knitted side is facing—one stitch has been wrapped and the yarn is correctly positioned to knit the next stitch. To hide the wrap on a subsequent purl row, work to the wrapped stitch, use the tip of the right needle to pick up the wrap from the back, place it on the left needle **(Figure 3)**, then purl it together with the wrapped stitch.

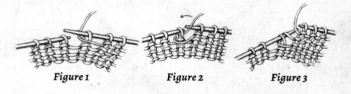

Figure 1   *Figure 2*   *Figure 3*

Sources for Yarn

Berroco
(401) 769-1212
berroco.com

Blue Moon Fiber Arts
bluemoonfiberarts.com

**Blue Sky Alpacas/
Spud & Chloë**
(763) 753-5815
spudandchloe.com

Brown Sheep Company
(800) 826-9136
brownsheep.com

Cascade Yarns
cascadeyarns.com

Classic Elite Yarns
(800) 343-0308
classiceliteyarns.com

**ColorSong Yarn/
Hand Maiden**
(541) 929-2359
colorsongyarn.com

Crafts Americana/KnitPicks
(800) 574-1323
knitpicks.com

**Fairmount Fibers/
Manos del Uruguay**
fairmountfibers.com

Harrisville Designs
(603) 827-3996
harrisville.com

Imperial Yarn
(541) 395-2507
imperialyarn.com

**Kelbourne Woolens/
The Fibre Company**
(484) 368-3666
kelbournewoolens.com

Knitting Fever/Debbie Bliss
(516) 546-3600
knittingfever.com

Lorna's Laces
(773) 935-3803
lornaslaces.net

Malabrigo
(786) 866-6187
malabrigoyarn.com

Madelinetosh
(817) 249-3066
madelinetosh.com

Patons
(800) 351-8357
patonsyarns.com

Plymouth Yarn Company
(215) 788-0459
plymouthyarn.com

Shibui Knits
(503) 595-5898
shibuiknits.com

Skacel/Zitron Lifestyle
(800) 255-1278
skacelknitting.com

Swans Island
(888) 526-9526
swansislandblankets.com

Three Irish Girls
threeirishgirls.com

Universal Yarn
(877) 864-9276
universalyarn.com

Westminster Fibers/Rowan
(800) 445-9276
westminsterfibers.com

Wooly Wonka Fibers
woolywonkafiber.com

Index